The
Country
Innkeepers'
Cookbook

♥

The
Country
Innkeepers'
Cookbook

Wilf & Lois Copping

Illustrated by Ray Maher

The Country Innkeepers' Cookbook
© 1992 by Wilf & Lois Copping
All rights reserved.
(Original copyright 1978 by Yankee Publishing Incorporated)

Published by Country Roads Press
P.O. Box 286, Lower Main Street
Castine, Maine 04421

Cover art by Victoria Sheridan.
Text design by Carl F. Kirkpatrick.
Library of Congress Catalog Card No. 92-074911
ISBN 1-56626-015-9

First Edition. Eleventh Printing, 1992.
Printed in the United States of America.

♥

DEDICATION

Lois: "I dedicate this book to Wilf."
Wilf: "I dedicate this book to Lois."

IN APPRECIATION

This book could never have been written without the help of a lot of other people. We won't name them as they do in the Oscar Awards or the Miss America Contest, to meaningless excess, but give thanks we will — to everybody who helped make this book possible. *They* know who they are.

CONTENTS

EDITOR'S NOTE

It was in the 1950s. The Coppings were both in New York, Wilf with an advertising agency, Lois with a publishing firm — at least she was before she retired to mother two sons.

They had long since renounced big city living in favor of a retreat in the wilds of Fairfield County, Connecticut — in a house that Wilf had somehow found time to build with his own two hands. It seemed like an idyllic existence, at least for Wilf, the glamor of New York by day, the peace and quiet of country living by night.

There was only one problem. To enjoy all this Wilf had to commute over 65 miles a day, *each way*. And he had been doing it for over six years.

Wilf: "I'd try to do all my homework on the train so that my evenings — what were left of them — would be free and clear. But even at that, by the time I got home the boys were ready for bed. In summer Lois and I might have time for one martini on the patio before dinner. In winter I'd generally make it home just in time to meet myself getting up in the morning."

Lois: "It was a rough life for all of us. We didn't see much of each other — or anybody else — until the weekends. Then we made up for it. We had a few good friends in the area whose lifestyle was much like our own and we all tried to outdo each other in the entertainment department. Fortunately we both liked to cook, and we hosted a dinner party almost every other Saturday night."

It was one such dinner party that got them thinking about the inn business.

Wilf: "We were all sitting around talking about what we'd rather be doing than what we *were* doing when a neighbor who had inherited a big old barn of a house said: 'Do you know what I think we should do? I think we should turn my place into a restaurant. It's big enough. There isn't a good place to eat for miles around. And if half the people here tonight would patronize us we'd have it made. The Coppings can do the cooking. We'll do everything else. What do you say?'

"We said 'no,' but the seed had been planted. To commute no more ... to leave the rat race ... to live in the country ... to have our own business and be our own boss. Heaven.

"We thought about it. We talked about it. Then, two years later, we did it. We sold our house. I quit my job. And we went into the inn business in Vermont."

To find just the place they were looking for, the Coppings went through the usual routine. They advertised. They read all the real estate ads. They contacted real estate agents. They drove all over New England. And they found just what they were looking for by accident.

"Did you see a FOR SALE sign in that tree?" asked Wilf as they drove along Route 11. They weren't even looking for real estate at this point. They were looking for a place to eat.

"I thought I did," answered Lois. "Let's turn back and check it out."

And sure enough there it was, a crude handmade FOR SALE sign half hidden in an old elm. Beneath it a little bridge crossed a stream. Beyond was a meadow and beyond that, a mountain. Pure Vermont.

At the end of the long lane they found the farmhouse, sheds and barns. A small field held several cows which looked up and stared. The scene was right out of Currier and Ives.

They looked around and then looked at each other. And they both knew: this was it.

The Coppings bought the place on the spot. They never checked the foundations or the roof or the sewage system or the water or any of the other things you're supposed to check before buying a property.

You fall in love, you don't ask any questions.

"What we went through to turn Deer Hill Farm into Deer Hill Inn would make Mr. Blandings blanch. We had to find space in each bedroom for a private bath. Old Vermont farmhouses don't have many bathrooms. We had to install a new heating system. We had to re-wire the whole house. We took a large carriage house, turned it into a playroom and joined it to the main house. We painted and decorated. We furnished. And we mortgaged. Especially we mortgaged. Then the well went dry. But it didn't matter. Nothing mattered. We were in a dream world doing our own thing and it was probably the happiest time of our lives."

The dream lasted five years. Deer Hill Inn was too small to make much money. And it got too big for the Coppings to run alone. They served breakfast, lunch and dinner to their guests and did most of the work themselves. They cooked. They washed dishes. They served. They cleaned up. They bartended. They *had* to. A small inn can't afford to pay professional help. In a small 'Ma and Pa' business the family does everything.

So Deer Hill Inn was sold and turned into a private estate.

But better things were in the offing —

The Windham Foundation was looking for a couple to run The Old Tavern at Grafton, Vermont, an authentic old stagecoach inn originally built in 1801 and restored with tender loving care by The Windham Foundation.

In rural Vermont, where everybody knows everybody else and everything that's going on, it didn't take long for The Windham Foundation and the Coppings to get together and in no time at all they were back in the inn business.

Things were different at The Old Tavern than at Deer Hill Inn. Different — and a lot better. At Deer Hill the Coppings were both captain *and* crew. At The Old Tavern they spent more time on the bridge, where they managed, directed, supervised. But they still planned the menus, supervised their preparation, and today are still at home behind the range.

AUTHORS' NOTE

Somebody was first — who, we will never know. But somebody, somewhere, sometime, while swinging by his tail or hunched on all fours, committed to trunk-of-tree, wall-of-cave, or sands-of-time, the very first recipe: "Take one Brontosaurus egg ..." or possibly it was, "Take one large, ripe banana ..." Since then it's never stopped. Cooks both good and bad have been originating, improvising, modifying, and sometimes improving recipes ever since.

Consider the output. Consider the number of recipes that have appeared in women's service magazines and newspapers. And the cookbooks. How many have been published? How many new ones are launched each year?

Browse through the cookery shelves of any well-stocked bookstore or library. In addition to the dozens of standard works you'll find cookbooks representing most every country, race, creed, color and ethnic group you ever heard of.

There are local cookbooks, regional cookbooks, seasonal cookbooks and "specialty" cookbooks beyond description. There are cookbooks promoting the use of specific foods: cranberries, chutney, cottage cheese, wheat germ, gelatin. And there are cookbooks that tell you how to cook with specific equipment: pressure cooker, blender, fondue pot, crock pot, wok, hibachi, radar range. If there is not now, there most certainly soon will be *Cooking with ESP — The Thought Range.*

Volumes have been written to meet the gourmet needs of the hiker, camper, backpacker, trailer, motor home and boating set. Look for: *Flambéeing for Flagpole Sitters, Barbecuing for Mountain Climbers, Sautéeing for Skin and Sky Divers.* Can't find them? Wait.

There's an aphrodisiac cookbook. Properly illustrated, one could probably produce an X-rated cookbook. (But it's far too late for a banned-in-Boston cookbook. Pity.) Is there no end to it? We doubt it. In the eons gone by since our ancestors crawled from the primordial ooze, we still eat the same basic foods. There's nothing new, never will be. Animal, vegetable, mineral. That's it.

But — consider the combinations and the variations. The different cooking methods. The infinite possibilities with seasonings and flavorings, herbs and spices. And consider the number of meals required to feed just one individual in his or her lifetime. Clearly the flow of recipes will never end. It will never end as long as we seek The Holy Grail, The Golden Fleece, The Great White Whale, The Lost Chord, The Fountain of Youth. Your reach as a cook should exceed your grasp, or what's a cookbook for?

INTRODUCTION

All the recipes in this book are *good* — all have been tried and proven in our Inns many times over. Everybody always likes them. There's no guesswork involved. If you cook for family and friends, these recipes will help make every meal a success and enhance your reputation as a host or hostess. If you're in the restaurant business you'll be happy to know that every one is a best-seller. To put it another way: dishes in this book are here because wherever and whenever served, they have always elicited the same flattering response: "May I have the recipe?" If you can boil water, fry an egg, make a sandwich, you can prepare any one of them.

People will ask *you* for recipes if you remember ...

COMPATIBILITY

You're not in this world very long before you realize that, due to Kismet, charm or charisma, you get along much better with some people than others. Hence the success of many relationships where the proper rapport is present — and the dismal failure where it isn't.

So it is with food. Some foods go together eminently well, others not at all. And the specific merits of each dish have nothing to do with it: Ham and Eggs, Pork and Beans, Macaroni and Cheese, Gin and Vermouth. What magic is created here? Why are these unions so great? Who knows? But it certainly behooves all of us to seek the many wonders of "taste-togetherness" that must exist but remain as yet undiscovered.

Remember, we eat with our eyes first. So a plate of food, when set on the table, should look as appealing as possible. You might even begin with the plate itself. It should be neutral in color and design. If too busy it will fight with the food. Plates with pictures or complicated designs belong on a plate rail or in a china cabinet. Or they should be used only as service plates.

As for the food itself, aim for colorful combinations. Happily, the more colors the more nutrition. Wasn't that nice of Mother Nature?

Consider texture, too. The way foods feel in the mouth is as important as the way they look and taste. So utilize the "crunch" of lightly-done carrots, the "rolypoly" feel of peas, the "flowery" tickle of broccoli. And vary the way you cut your vegetables — slice them across, lengthwise, diagonally. Serve them whole, halved, diced, diamond-shaped. Do all you can to keep up appearances!

Combination of textures is another way to add interest. And the possibilities are infinite. The addition of a few raw crisp vegetables does a lot for cottage cheese. Aren't nuts and croutons good in a salad? And raisins and dates in hot cereal? Ice cream is a universal favorite. So is hot apple pie. But aren't they great together? And aren't tangy chunks of pineapple in gelatin more interesting than soft, bland slices of banana?

So in the interest of good taste, make sure everything you serve goes well together.

HERBS AND SPICES

Herbs and spices can also help you on your way to becoming a great cook; they equal flavoring and flavoring equals taste. And that's what good food is all about. Taste.

That doesn't mean we think you should start lacing every dish with mace, saffron, tarragon and turmeric. All seasoning (and all cooking) should be subtle. Natural flavors should be enhanced, not masked. Think of seasoning as background music. You'd miss it if it weren't there, but it never dominates. (If the first thing you notice about a woman is perfume, she's wearing too much of it!)

But first discover the taste of food, properly cooked,

with no flavoring at all, except just what Nature put in. You'll be surprised — and impressed.

WINES, ETC.

The French, certainly among the world's greatest cooks, consider *wine* a basic ingredient and use it in everything from soup to dessert. Take the wine away from a French chef and you take away the essence of his craft.

We've never been in a restaurant kitchen that wasn't equipped with at least a bottle of sherry. In most, some Madeira, claret and Burgundy were also in evidence, along with white wine, brandy and a few liqueurs. And rarely will you find a good restaurant that doesn't serve wine, unless it's in one of those unfortunate "dry" localities. The simple fact is that wine makes food taste better — both in the cooking and in the eating.

The increase in wine sales during the past few years indicates that more and more people are using wine for the same reasons the professionals do: to tenderize meats, to add flavor to food and zest to the appetite, to make ordinary dishes uncommonly good. Wine makes the meal — and the guests — seem more "special" somehow. There are many recipes in this book where wine is used. Beer has a place in good cooking too; there are those who hold that a genuine Welsh Rabbit cannot be made without it.

Cooking with spirits is easy and relatively inexpensive because you don't use much. And don't worry about the alcoholic content — that evaporates in the cooking process, leaving only the flavor and aroma to enjoy. Of course, not all wines are good for cooking, and not all dishes are improved by them, so exercise caution just as with herbs and spices.

ONE LAST WORD: LEFTOVERS

In general, we don't believe in them. A good restaurant chef rarely has any to begin with. He may roast an additional rib on Sunday because he wants hash on Monday. He may cook extra chicken on Tuesday because he plans chicken pie on Wednesday. And on Thursday he may boil up more spuds than usual because Friday's menu calls for potato pancakes. But that's good planning, not leftovers.

Remember that once cooked, vegetables are hardly worth serving again. They'll have little flavor or food value. If you can't bring yourself to throw them out, add to soup. After a few days in the refrigerator most cooked meat will be dry and tasteless. If you feel you must use it up, make a stew. And an old fish is about as appealing as it sounds. Feed to the cat.

Around the fourth day, better throw it out, whatever it is. Just taking up space and about ready to spoil.

In short, we believe the best way to use leftovers is to plan not to have any in the first place.

Now — on to the recipes. Good luck and good eating!

We may live without poetry, music and art,
We may live without conscience and live without heart,
We may live without friends,
We may live without books,
But civilized man cannot live without cooks.

Owen Meredith

APPETIZERS
Canapés, Hors d'Oeuvres, or Antipasto

Whatever you call them, remember: the purpose is to stimulate and arouse the appetite, not stultify it.

But a platter of well-designed and well-prepared nibble-food is difficult, if not impossible, to resist. And many guests, not knowing or caring what may follow, are apt to indulge themselves to the limit.

The same goes for cocktails, which should whet the appetite, not drown it. After several rounds, some drinkers won't know the difference between a Beef Wellington and a frozen meat pie, which gives small satisfaction to the cook who may have spent the best part of the day in the kitchen.

If you've taken a lot of time and trouble preparing a meal, you want your guests to appreciate it. So go easy on the preliminaries. That's not to say you must let down on the *quality*. You can exercise just as much creativity and skill here as with the main course. Just watch the *quantity*. Don't make too many, and don't pass them around too often.

ARTICHOKES WITH ZIPPY DIP

Ah, the elegant artichoke!

6 medium-size artichokes

Trim stems from artichokes. Lay each on its side and cut off 1 inch from the top. Trim off the spiny tips of the leaves with scissors. Wash under running water.

Stand the artichokes upright in a large saucepan; pour in water to a depth of 1 inch. Simmer, covered, for about 40 minutes or until tender when pierced with a fork. Drain well.

Serve with Zippy Dip (see below). *Serves 6.*

ZIPPY DIP

½ cup mayonnaise
1 teaspoon dry mustard
1 teaspoon fresh lemon juice

BLUE CHEESE BALL

Your guests will hesitate to break into this elegant-looking creation, but once they start there'll be no stopping them. Spreads very easily.

½ pound blue cheese
½ cup apple juice
4 tablespoons butter
½ cup toasted chopped almonds

Crumble the cheese in a small bowl and cover with apple juice; refrigerate overnight. Drain off the juice and mix the cheese with butter until smooth.

Shape into a ball and sprinkle all over with almonds. Chill. Remove from the refrigerator one hour before serving, and let stand at room temperature.

Serve as a spread for Melba toast or small pieces of crusty French bread. *Serves 4-6.*

HOT CHEESE TOASTIES

You should always offer at least one hot canapé, and this one isn't too hard to make.

6 slices bacon, cooked until crisp and
  crumbled
1½ tablespoons butter
1½ tablespoons flour
½ cup milk
1 cup sharp cheddar cheese, grated
1 small onion, grated
1 egg
¼ teaspoon salt
1 tablespoon green pepper, grated
⅛ teaspoon dry mustard
¼ teaspoon Worcestershire sauce
8 slices firm white bread, crusts
  removed

Melt the butter over low heat. Add the flour and blend, stirring constantly, for 4 minutes. Stir in the milk and cook until thick and smooth. Blend in the cheese, onion and bacon.

Beat the egg; add salt, green pepper, mustard and Worcestershire sauce and add to the first mixture.

Toast the bread on one side, turn and butter lightly, and toast on other side. Spread each slice with the mixture. Divide into three strips. Place the strips on a cookie sheet. Broil for 3 or 4 minutes or until lightly browned. Serve at once. *Makes 24 canapés.*

CHEESE WAFERS

Far superior to the expensive crackers you buy. Make these up and just keep them in the refrigerator until ready to bake.

½ pound sharp cheddar cheese, grated
4 tablespoons butter
¾ cup flour
⅛ teaspoon Tabasco sauce
½ teaspoon salt

Cream cheese thoroughly with butter and add the flour. Add seasonings and form into a roll one inch in diameter. Wrap the roll in wax paper and chill thoroughly.

To bake, cut the roll in slices ⅛ inch thick. Bake in a 475°F oven for 8 minutes or until golden brown.

Makes 4 dozen wafers.

CLAM DIP

You can buy dips that sound very much like this one, but why not put it together yourself and save the money? Tastes better, too.

1 3-ounce package cream cheese,
   softened
1 7-ounce can minced clams
½ pint sour cream
⅛ teaspoon Worcestershire sauce
2 tablespoons onion juice
2 tablespoons lemon juice

Drain the clams, reserving some of the liquid, and mash into the softened cream cheese. Add the remaining ingredients and blend well.

If a thinner dip is required, use 1 or 2 tablespoons of the reserved clam liquid to thin the mixture.

Serve with corn or potato chips. *Makes 2 cups.*

CRABMEAT CANAPES

For people who like curry — and for people who just think they don't like it.

> 12 slices white bread
> 1½ cups mayonnaise
> 1½ teaspoons curry powder
> 1½ cups cooked crabmeat, canned or frozen
> 1 cup shredded cheddar cheese

Cut two rounds from each slice of bread. Toast on one side. Mix the curry and mayonnaise and spread on untoasted sides. Add one tablespoon crabmeat. Sprinkle cheese on top. Toast under the broiler until golden brown.

Makes 24 canapés.

CUCUMBER SURPRISE

If you have the patience to hollow out cucumbers (use a sharp knife or apple-corer), this will add considerable interest to any tray of canapés.

> 2 firm, medium-size cucumbers
> 1 3-ounce package cream cheese
> 1 teaspoon dry beef base
> ¼ teaspoon Worcestershire sauce
> 4 drops Tabasco sauce

Combine the cheese, beef base, Worcestershire sauce and Tabasco sauce and blend well. Stuff into the centers of peeled, hollowed-out cucumbers. Chill for 2 hours.

Slice into rounds and serve on crisp crackers.

Makes 24 canapés.

DEVILED EGGS

Deviled eggs are a cocktail party staple, but the ham in these makes them deliciously different.

12 eggs
1 small can deviled ham
¼ teaspoon dry mustard
3 or 4 tablespoons mayonnaise

Hard cook the eggs, remove from shells and cut lengthwise into halves. Remove the yolks and mash with a fork. Add ham, mustard and mayonnaise (enough to make mixture creamy) to the yolks and mix until smooth. Fill the whites with the egg yolk mixture.

12 servings.

GUACAMOLE SPREAD

Has a delicate, nutty flavor and a smooth, buttery texture.

1 large ripe avocado
1 tablespoon lime juice
1 teaspoon Worcestershire sauce
½ teaspoon salt
½ teaspoon finely grated onion
½ teaspoon garlic salt
⅛ teaspoon cayenne pepper

Cut the avocado in half and remove the seed, then peel. Sprinkle immediately with lime juice and mash well with a fork. Add the other ingredients and mix well. Cover and chill in the refrigerator for one hour. Serve in a small bowl surrounded by Melba toast. *Makes 1 cup.*

PATE

Easy to make, keeps well, and tastes delicious.

1 pound chicken livers
1 teaspoon salt

¼ pound bulk sausage
1 small onion, grated
1 teaspoon lemon juice
¼ teaspoon salt
⅛ teaspoon freshly ground black pepper
1½ tablespoons heavy cream
1½ tablespoons cognac

Simmer the chicken livers in a quart of boiling water seasoned with 1 teaspoon salt for 4 minutes. Drain, cool and remove the membrane. Cut the livers into small pieces and grind in a meat grinder. Add the onion, lemon juice, salt and pepper.

Fry the sausage until thoroughly cooked and add to the liver mixture. Beat in the cream and cognac. Chill for an hour or two and serve with crackers.   *Makes 3 cups.*

SALMON BALL

Every bit as impressive as the Blue Cheese Ball on page 24. If you're having a big enough party, serve them both.

1 1-pound can red salmon
1 8-ounce package cream cheese
1 tablespoon lemon juice
1 teaspoon horseradish
2 teaspoons onion, grated
¼ teaspoon salt
⅛ teaspoon Tabasco sauce
½ cup walnuts, chopped
3 tablespoons parsley, minced

Soften the cream cheese. Drain and flake the salmon. Mix these two together, beating well. Add the lemon juice, horseradish, onion, salt and Tabasco. Chill for 4 hours.

Form into a ball, roll in nuts and parsley mixed together. Chill again before serving with crisp crackers.
About 12 servings.

MEXICAN SEVICHE

A very unusual dish, but it's not really raw as many people think; enzymes in the lime juice perform a kind of pre-digestive or cooking process.

    2 pounds very fresh, firm-fleshed fish
    2 cups lime juice
    1 cup tomato juice
    1 onion, finely chopped
  ¼ cup finely chopped parsley
    2 tablespoons finely chopped green
       pepper
  ½ cup sliced pimiento-stuffed olives
    1 teaspoon salt

Cut the raw fish in bite-size pieces and pour the lime juice over it. Use a glass dish, covered, and refrigerate for 4 hours.

Drain the fish and add other ingredients. Refrigerate overnight to blend flavors. Serve with crackers or tortillas.   *About 4 cups.*

PARTY SHRIMP

It's the beer that makes it taste so special. Be sure not to overcook the shrimp or they'll be tough.

    1 pound shrimp, medium size, in shell
    1 12-ounce can beer
  ½ teaspoon thyme
  ½ teaspoon dry mustard
    1 bay leaf
    1 clove garlic, minced

1½ teaspoons salt
1 tablespoon chopped parsley
1 teaspoon chopped onion

Put all the ingredients in a pot and bring to a boil, then reduce the heat immediately. Simmer 3 minutes or until the shrimp turn pink. Cool the shrimp in the liquid, then shell and devein. Chill and serve with Cocktail Sauce (see below).   *Serves 4.*

COCKTAIL SAUCE

½ cup chili sauce
1 tablespoon prepared horseradish
2 teaspoons lemon juice
1 teaspoon Worcestershire sauce
dash Tabasco sauce

Mix together and chill before serving.

SHRIMP PUFFS

They have an intriguing, "melt-in-the-mouth" quality that you'll find quite delicious.

24 small shrimp, cooked, shelled and
    deveined
1 egg white
¼ cup sharp cheddar cheese, grated
⅛ teaspoon salt
⅛ teaspoon paprika
½ cup mayonnaise
24 slices round party rye bread

Beat the egg white until stiff. Fold in the cheese, salt, paprika and mayonnaise.

Heap this mixture on the party rye rounds. Top each round with one shrimp. Broil the puffs until light brown. Serve hot.   *Makes 24 canapés.*

SHRIMP REMOULADE

Planning a very special dinner? Try this for openers.

1½ pounds cooked, shelled and
   deveined shrimp
1 cup mayonnaise
½ cup seeded, chopped cucumber
2 tablespoons chopped parsley
2 tablespoons chopped chives
1 tablespoon horseradish
½ teaspoon dry mustard
2 teaspoons lemon juice
½ teaspoon salt

Chill the shrimp. Mix the remaining ingredients together and chill.

Just before serving, mix the sauce with the shrimp and place on crisp lettuce. *Serves 4-5.*

MINIATURE SHRIMP TURNOVERS

These require a little effort, but they're worth it. Make in advance and heat up later. Good when you're hosting VIP's.

THE TURNOVERS

1½ cups water
2 tablespoons butter
1½ cups flour
1 teaspoon salt

Place the water and butter in a saucepan and heat to boiling. Add the flour and salt all at once, stirring vigorously over low heat until the mixture forms a ball and leaves the sides of the pan clean. Cover and let cool to room temperature.

THE FILLING

> 3 tablespoons olive oil or butter
> 1 medium onion, finely chopped
> 1 pound raw shrimp, shelled, deveined
> and finely chopped
> 2 eggs, lightly beaten
> ½ teaspoon salt
> ⅛ teaspoon ground black pepper
> 2 tablespoons chopped parsley

Heat the oil or butter and sauté the onion in it until tender and lightly browned. Add the chopped shrimp and cook, stirring, for 2 or 3 minutes or until the shrimp turn pink. Stir in the beaten eggs, salt and pepper and cook, stirring, until eggs are just set.

Stir in the parsley and let cool to room temperature.

*   *   *

Knead the cooled dough on a lightly-floured board until smooth and elastic. Divide into two parts. Roll out one-half of the dough until it is very thin. Cut out 3-inch circles. Place one-half teaspoon of filling on each circle, moisten the edges, and fold over to make a turnover. Pinch the edges to seal.

> 2 eggs, lightly beaten
> 2½ cups dried bread crumbs

Coat the turnovers, first in the above two beaten eggs, then in bread crumbs. Fry five or six at a time in deep fat preheated to 355°F until golden, about 3 minutes. Drain on paper towels.

Repeat with the second half of the dough and remaining filling. *Makes 80 bite-size turnovers.*

TUNA AND CHEESE CANAPES

The tuna makes it inexpensive, and the vermouth makes it fancy.

        1 cup grated cheddar cheese
        ½ cup flaked tuna fish
        2 tablespoons dry vermouth
        6 slices white bread, crusts removed

Toast the bread lightly and cut each slice in four. Combine cheese, tuna fish and vermouth and blend well. Spread on toast.

Bake in a 350°F oven for 5 minutes. *Makes 24 canapés.*

COCKTAIL PLATTER

Calorie counters and health food devotees go to cocktail parties too, and they will appreciate these goodies.

        1 medium-size red cabbage
        1 medium-size cucumber
        1 green pepper
        1 small cauliflower
        6 small carrots
        1 bunch celery
       12 radishes

Hollow out the cabbage and place in the center of a large platter. Surround with iced cucumber strips, green pepper slices, cauliflower florets, carrot sticks, celery sticks and radishes.

Make a dip by mixing together the following ingredients and fill the center of the hollowed-out cabbage:

        1 cup mayonnaise
        ½ cup sour cream
        ¼ cup minced onion
        1 tablespoon anchovy paste
        1 clove garlic, minced
        dash pepper

Should be enough for 4-8, depending on what else you serve.

SURPRISE BITES

(The surprise comes when you bite into them and find an olive.)

> 36 small stuffed olives
> 2 cups sharp cheddar cheese, finely grated
> ½ cup soft butter
> 1 cup flour
> ¼ teaspoon Tabasco sauce
> ½ teaspoon salt
> 1 teaspoon paprika

Blend the cheese and butter until well mixed. Stir in the flour, salt, paprika and Tabasco and blend well. Wrap one teaspoon of dough around each olive, covering it completely.

Arrange on a cookie sheet and bake in a 400°F oven for 15 minutes. Serve hot. *Makes 36 canapés.*

SOUPS

"Soup of the evening, beautiful Soup!
Who would not give all else for two p
ennyworth only of beautiful Soup?"

Lewis Carroll, *Alice in Wonderland*

There is an aura of mysticism surrounding soup. And there is no easier way to earn a reputation as a cook than to learn how to make a good one. We know a gentleman who travels in a very sophisticated circle, and he ranks 'way up there with Escoffier in the minds of his peers. He can't cook for beans. All he does is invite friends in once in a while for a big bowl of soup. But it's a good one.

The curative powers of soup, particularly chicken soup, baffle medical science. Serve a good soup at a progressive dinner, and you'll earn many more plaudits than you deserve (to the dismay of your friend who spent all day on a fancy pâté). And of course, any great meal is described as having everything "from soup to nuts." The soup has to be there. The nuts don't.

The secret of good soup is in the stock. So extract and save the goodness from bones that normally go in the garbage. And keep the vegetable water instead of dumping it down the drain. If this all poses too much of a problem for you, use canned broth or consommé. Or buy a commercial base.

If you must use canned soups, dress them up a bit. Most people can recognize an unadorned canned soup from across the room, which won't help your reputation one whit. Ordinary canned tomato soup is vastly improved by a dollop of sour cream or whipped cream; a lentil soup by the addition of a few thin slices of lemon; a cream of chicken soup garnished with a diced apple soaked in lemon juice.

Consider *compatibility* when you put soup on the menu, too. Don't serve a thick pea soup with roast pork and beans; serve a consommé. Don't serve a broth with a main-course chef's salad; serve a fisherman's chowder. And sure, hot soups are good in winter and cold soups are nice in summer. But if your dining room is well heated, try a cold cucumber soup some January along with barbecued pot roast. And isn't it possible that people who go for hot tea in July might also appreciate hot soup once in a while?

Few areas offer as much opportunity for your imagination to roam as does soup. And few other cries are as welcome as "Soup's on!"

CHILLED AVOCADO SOUP

A hot-day soup.

> 2 ripe avocados, peeled and pitted
> 1 tablespoon dry sherry
> 1 quart chilled chicken stock
> ½ cup light cream
> ½ teaspoon salt
> ⅛ teaspoon cayenne pepper
> ½ cup sour cream
> paprika

Blend all ingredients except the sour cream and paprika in the electric blender until smooth.

Chill 4 hours. Serve topped with sour cream and a sprinkling of paprika.   *6 servings.*

CHILLED BEET SOUP

The buttermilk in this soup gives it a particularly pleasing and tangy flavor.

> 1 cup tomato juice
> 2 cups chopped, cooked beets
> 1 quart fresh buttermilk
> 1½ teaspoons salt
> ¼ teaspoon pepper
> 3 tablespoons chopped fresh chives *or*
>   6-8 thin slices of cucumber

Combine the tomato juice, beets, salt and pepper in blender. Blend until smooth and add the buttermilk. Chill for 3-4 hours. Garnish with chives or cucumber slices.   *6-8 servings.*

CHILLED BLUEBERRY SOUP

In some European countries, fruit soups are served as a dessert, but our guests seem to prefer them as a prelude to dinner.

 2½ cups fresh blueberries
 1 tablespoon cornstarch
 2 cups cold water
 2 tablespoons sugar
 1½ cups Marsala wine
 ½ cup sour cream

Blend the cornstarch with a little of the cold water; then add the rest of the water, blueberries, sugar and Marsala wine. Simmer for about 10 minutes, or until the blueberries are soft. Whirl in blender until smooth or put the mixture through a food mill. Cool.

Stir in the sour cream. Serve well-chilled. *8 servings.*

CREAM OF CARROT SOUP

. . . in which the lowly carrot proves to be star material.

 8 carrots
 2 stalks celery, chopped
 1 bay leaf
 3 cups chicken broth
 ½ teaspoon salt
 ⅛ teaspoon freshly ground pepper
 ¾ cup heavy cream
 1 egg yolk, beaten

Scrape the carrots and slice them. Combine with the celery, bay leaf, chicken broth, salt and pepper. Bring to a boil and simmer until the carrots are tender. Do not overcook. Remove the bay leaf.

Force the mixture through a food mill or purée in an electric blender. Return the mixture to the saucepan and bring to a boil. Remove from heat and add the heavy cream and egg yolk. Reheat but do not boil. *4-6 servings.*

CHILLED CHERRY SOUP

Pretty and refreshing. Serve either as a soup or dessert.

    1 1-pound can red sour pitted cherries,
         including liquid
    ¼ cup sugar
    2 teaspoons cornstarch
    ¼ teaspoon salt
    ¼ teaspoon cinnamon
    2 teaspoons grated orange rind
    ½ cup orange juice
    ½ cup red burgundy wine

Blend in the blender all ingredients except the wine for 20 seconds. Pour the mixture into a saucepan and cook over medium heat, stirring constantly, until it comes to a boil. Boil for 1 minute, stirring.

Remove from the heat and stir in the wine. Chill overnight or for at least 12 hours.

Serve garnished with whipped cream or sour cream.

4 servings.

CREAM OF CORN SOUP

When we had our own inn in Vermont, we ran a buffet every Saturday night, and this soup was always on it. If it wasn't, people complained — that's how good it is.

4 tablespoons butter
1 medium-size onion, chopped
4 tablespoons flour
2 cups milk
2½ cups coffee cream
1½ teaspoons salt
⅛ teaspoon white pepper
3¾ cups cream-style canned corn
4 tablespoons fresh parsley, chopped

Melt the butter and sauté the chopped onion until yellow. Stir in the flour. Add milk and cream, stirring until smooth and thickened. Add corn, salt and pepper and heat to the simmering point. Do not boil.

Sprinkle parsley on top just before serving. *8 servings.*

CHILLED CUCUMBER SOUP

Most *refreshing on a hot summer day!*

2 medium-size cucumbers
4 cups chicken broth, boiling
1 cup sour cream
1 tablespoon minced onion
1 teaspoon grated lemon rind
⅛ teaspoon garlic powder
1½ tablespoons chopped fresh
    parsley

Peel the cucumbers and remove the seeds. Dice. Add

to boiling chicken broth. Simmer for 10 minutes, then cool.

Purée the cucumber-broth mixture in the blender. Add sour cream and blend well. Stir in the minced onion, lemon rind and garlic powder. If necessary, add salt and pepper to taste.

Chill the soup until frosty cold. Serve in chilled bowls. Sprinkle with parsley. *6 servings.*

GAZPACHO

A classic Spanish soup.

> 4 pounds tomatoes, peeled and diced
> 1 medium-size cucumber, diced
> 1 green pepper, chopped
> ½ large onion, chopped
> 1 clove garlic, minced
> 1 cup soft bread crumbs
> 2 cups water
> ½ teaspoon cayenne pepper
> 1 tablespoon salt
> 1½ teaspoons olive oil
> ¾ cup vinegar
> ¼ cup pimiento-stuffed olives, chopped
> ¼ cup parsley, chopped
> ¼ cup celery, chopped fine

Combine tomatoes, cucumbers, green peppers, onion, garlic, bread crumbs and water. Bring to boiling. Cover and simmer 1 hour. Force through sieve or food mill. Add pepper, salt, oil and vinegar. Mix well. Chill thoroughly. Serve with olives, parsley and celery as toppings. *6 servings.*

LEMONY LENTIL SOUP

If you're tempted to add sliced frankfurters to this soup, please don't.

> 2 cups lentils
> 6 cups water
> 1 large onion, sliced
> ¼ cup olive oil
> 1½ teaspoons salt
> 1 pound fresh spinach
> juice of 1 large lemon

Wash and drain the lentils. Cover with the water and simmer for 1½ hours. Sauté the onion in the olive oil until golden. Add the onion and oil to the lentils and stir in the salt. Cook gently for one hour.

Wash the spinach thoroughly and chop up, not too fine, and add to the lentils. Simmer for 15 minutes and then stir in the lemon juice.

Serve with a paper-thin slice of lemon in each bowl.

6 servings.

MEATBALL SOUP

Hearty and satisfying.

> ½ pound ground beef
> ½ cup quick-cooking oats
> ¼ cup finely chopped onion
> ¼ cup finely chopped parsley
> 2¼ quarts chicken broth
> ⅓ cup lemon juice
> 3 eggs
> salt and pepper

Combine the beef, oats, onion and parsley. Form into small balls the size of a walnut. Heat the broth to boiling and drop in the meatballs. Simmer, covered, for 45 minutes.

Just before serving, combine the eggs and lemon juice and beat until thoroughly blended. Remove the meatballs from liquid and distribute among 8 to 10 soup bowls. Slowly pour the broth into the egg mixture, beating constantly. Add salt and pepper to taste at this point. Pour over the meatballs and serve immediately.

8-10 servings.

CREAM OF MUSHROOM SOUP

Please do not use anything but fresh mushrooms and butter in this.

>   1 pound fresh mushrooms
>   1 small onion, chopped
>   4 tablespoons butter
>   1 cup chicken stock
>   4 tablespoons butter
>   3 tablespoons flour
>   2 cups milk or light cream
>   ½ teaspoon salt
>   ⅛ teaspoon pepper
>   1½ cups sour cream

Sauté the mushrooms and chopped onion in 4 tablespoons of butter. Cook slowly for 20 minutes, stirring regularly. Add chicken stock.

Melt over low heat the other 4 tablespoons butter. Add the flour and cook for 5 minutes, stirring. Add milk or cream slowly and stir until thickened and smooth. Add salt and pepper. Stir in the mushrooms, onion and chicken stock. Slowly add the sour cream, which has been brought to room temperature.

Serve garnished with fresh, chopped parsley. *4 servings.*

CREAM OF PEANUT SOUP

An old Southern favorite which is gaining popularity in the North.

> 1 medium onion, chopped
> 2 stalks celery, chopped
> 4 tablespoons butter
> 1 tablespoon flour
> 2 quarts chicken stock or canned chicken broth
> 1 cup smooth peanut butter
> 2 cups light cream
> ⅓ cup chopped peanuts

Sauté the onion and celery in butter until soft, but not brown. Stir in the flour and cook until bubbly. Add the chicken stock, stirring constantly, and bring to a boil. Remove the soup from the heat and rub through a sieve.

Add the peanut butter and cream, stirring to blend thoroughly. Return to low heat, but do not boil, and serve garnished with peanuts. *10-12 servings.*

POTATO ONION SOUP

A basic soup that sure hits the spot on a chilly day.

3 medium-size potatoes
3 medium-size onions
1 tablespoon flour
3 cups milk
¾ teaspoon salt
⅛ teaspoon pepper
2 tablespoons butter or margarine
2 eggs

Dice the potatoes and onions and cook until soft in water to cover. Do not drain. Mix the flour into cold milk and add to the onion-potato mixture. Simmer until the flour is cooked and the mixture has thickened. Add salt, pepper and butter. Remove from heat.

Beat the eggs until light yellow. Dribble the soup into eggs, stirring all the while. Do not boil after the eggs are added, or the soup will curdle.   *4 servings.*

PUMPKIN SOUP

We wish we had a dollar for every time we've handed out this recipe!

2 pounds fresh pumpkin
3 cups scalded coffee cream or milk
1 tablespoon butter
2 teaspoons maple syrup
1 teaspoon salt
⅛ teaspoon nutmeg

Steam the fresh pumpkin, then mash. (Three cups canned pumpkin may be substituted.)

Stir into the milk, then add the remaining ingredients. Heat, but do not boil, and serve immediately.

6-8 servings.

SPORTSMAN'S HEARTY SOUP

Serve it with a green salad, a chunk of dark bread and red wine. Now that's *a meal!*

2 pounds shin beef with bone
5 quarts cold water
2 tablespoons salt
1 cup dried lima beans
2 tablespoons salad or olive oil
3 cloves garlic, sliced
1 medium onion, minced
½ cup parsley, chopped
½ pound ground beef
⅓ teaspoon pepper
1 cup celery, diced
2 cups cabbage, shredded fine
1 cup carrots, diced
3½ cups canned tomatoes
1½ cups elbow macaroni
1 10-ounce package frozen peas

Place the shin beef with bone, water, salt, and beans in a large pot. Bring to a boil; skim. Cover and simmer for 2½ hours. Cool and refrigerate overnight.

The next day, sauté in oil the garlic, onion, parsley, ground beef and pepper until the onion is tender. Discard the garlic. Remove the bone from the soup and cut the meat into bite-size pieces. Add meat to the soup, along with the onion mixture, celery, cabbage, carrots and tomatoes. Simmer, covered, until the vegetables are tender.

Skim the fat from the soup. Add the macaroni and peas and cook, covered, for about 10 minutes. Add salt to taste.   *10 main-course servings.*

TOMATO SOUP

There doesn't seem to be anything special about this recipe, but all the ingredients come together somehow to produce a classic tomato soup. We've never tasted better.

3 cups peeled tomatoes, fresh or canned
 and drained
1 teaspoon baking soda
1 pint milk
½ teaspoon salt
⅛ teaspoon pepper
1 tablespoon butter

Bring the tomatoes to a boil and simmer for 10 minutes. Mash the tomatoes with a potato masher.

Add the baking soda. Let the foam subside and add milk, salt, pepper and butter.

Heat but do not boil, and serve immediately. *4 servings.*

SALADS AND
DRESSINGS

The ubiquitous restaurant salad bar has put the raw materials for a good salad in the hands of so many people that there is no longer any excuse for not learning how to build a good one.

For the same reason it is hard to be different in the salad department. But it's not hard to be *better*. Because a lot of people still ignore the basics and consistently turn out salads that are dull, limp and tasteless.

To produce a bright, interesting, crisp salad that's full of taste and eye appeal, you *must:*

use only fresh vegetables

wash them thoroughly

dry them completely

add the dressing at the last moment.

But after all's been said and done, it's the dressing that makes a different salad and a better salad. This is why you'll find more recipes in this chapter for salad dressings than salads. We go along with the old saw that says to make a great salad you need, "a patient man to do the preparation, a genius to make the dressing and a madman to do the mixing."

SUNSHINE SALAD

Refreshingly spring-like!

- 1 small head iceberg lettuce
- 1 medium-size ripe avocado, peeled and sliced
- 3 oranges, peeled and sectioned
- 1 grapefruit, peeled and sectioned
- 1 small red onion, sliced paper-thin and separated into rings
- Celery Seed Dressing (see page 62)

Line six small salad bowls (preferably glass) with lettuce leaves; break the remaining lettuce into bite-size pieces, dividing among the bowls. Arrange avocado slices, orange sections, grapefruit sections and onion rings on top of the lettuce in each bowl. Sprinkle each with about 1 tablespoon of Celery Seed Dressing and pass extra dressing when serving the salads. *6 servings.*

BORSCHT SALAD

Top this with sour cream and a sprinkling of dill.

- 1 20-ounce can crushed pineapple
- 1 6-ounce package black-cherry gelatin
- 1½ cups boiling water
- 1 16-ounce can shoestring beets
- 3 tablespoons vinegar
- 1 teaspoon dill weed
- ¼ teaspoon salt
- 1 cup chopped celery

Drain the pineapple, reserving syrup. Dissolve the gelatin in boiling water. Stir in the beets and beet liquid, vinegar, dill, salt and reserved pineapple syrup. Chill until the mixture thickens to the consistency of unbeaten egg white. Fold in the celery and pineapple. Pour into a 6-cup mold and chill until firm.   *8 servings.*

COTTAGE CHEESE MOLDED SALAD

Low in calories, high in nourishment — make it now, serve it later. Most attractive to look at and children like it, too.

1 tablespoon unflavored gelatin
¼ cup cold water
1 cup hot water
½ cup sugar
¼ teaspoon salt
½ cup lemon juice
1½ tablespoons vinegar
½ cup mayonnaise
⅛ teaspoon pepper
1 cup chopped raw spinach
¾ cup cottage cheese
⅓ cup diced celery
1 tablespoon chopped onion

Soak the gelatin in the ¼ cup of cold water. Dissolve it in the 1 cup hot water. Add the sugar and salt and stir until dissolved. Add the lemon juice, vinegar, mayonnaise and pepper. Blend with a rotary beater. Pour into a refrigerator tray and chill until firm one inch from the edge (about 25 minutes).

Whip with the beater until fluffy. Fold in the spinach, cottage cheese, celery and onion. Pour into individual molds and chill in the refrigerator for about 1 hour.

6 servings.

CRABMEAT DELIGHT

Can also be served as a spread.

  1 envelope unflavored gelatin
  3 tablespoons cold water
  1 can cream of mushroom soup
  6 ounces cream cheese, softened
  1 cup mayonnaise
  1 cup finely chopped celery
  1 small onion, minced
  1 cup crabmeat, cooked

Sprinkle gelatin over cold water to soften for about 5 minutes. Heat the soup to the boiling point and stir in the gelatin until dissolved. Cool.

Add the softened cream cheese, blending until smooth. Stir in the mayonnaise, celery and onion, mixing well. Fold in the crabmeat, which has been cut into bite-size pieces.

Pour into a ring mold and chill for 4 or 5 hours. Turn into a serving plate. Fill the center with ripe olives and garnish with watercress or chicory.   *6 servings.*

CRANBERRY CREAM SALAD

Very New England and very good for you. Has everything a salad should have — including lots of eye-appeal.

  1 1-pound can whole cranberry sauce
  2 teaspoons fresh lemon juice

1 cup sour cream
¼ cup confectioners' sugar
1 teaspoon vanilla
¾ cup chopped walnuts

Line ice-cube trays with transparent wrap. Stir lemon juice into the whole cranberry sauce and pour into the ice-cube trays. Combine the sour cream with the sugar, vanilla and nuts and spoon over the cranberry layer. Freeze, remove from the trays, and wrap for freezer. To serve, slice into eight portions and place on crisp lettuce. Fruit Salad Dressing on page 63 is good with this.

8 servings.

CRANBERRY GELATIN SALAD

Especially good with turkey; because of its lovely color, particularly appropriate at Christmas time.

1 3-ounce box raspberry gelatin
1 1-pound can whole cranberry sauce
1 large orange, sectioned and cut up
1 small can crushed pineapple
¼ cup chopped walnuts

Dissolve the gelatin in 1 cup boiling water, then add ½ cup of cold water. When the mixture begins to jell, add the cranberry sauce, orange, crushed pineapple and walnuts. Turn into a mold or individual molds and chill until firm.
8 servings.

CUCUMBER RELISH SALAD

The horseradish makes this a perfect accompaniment for roast beef or ham.

> 2 envelopes unflavored gelatin
> 1½ cups cold water
> 2 tablespoons instant minced onion
> 1½ teaspoons salt
> 2 teaspoons sugar
> 2 cups grated peeled cucumber
> 1 pint sour cream
> 4 tablespoons prepared horseradish
> 4 tablespoons vinegar

Soften the gelatin in cold water in a medium-size saucepan; stir in the instant onion, salt and sugar. Heat just to boiling. Remove from the heat, stir to dissolve the gelatin completely, and then stir in the grated cucumber, sour cream, horseradish and vinegar.

Pour into a mold; chill 4 hours or until firm. Unmold and garnish with cherry tomatoes and ripe olives.

6 servings.

CHILLED FRUIT SALAD LOAF

Very pretty and very good in the summer when you're having guests for lunch.

> 2 eggs, beaten
> 2 tablespoons vinegar
> 2 tablespoons sugar
> 2 tablespoons butter or margarine
> 1 cup whipped cream
> 2 cups green seedless grapes

2 cups diced, canned pineapple
2 oranges, cut up
2 medium bananas, sliced

Put the eggs in the top of a double boiler over hot water. Add the vinegar and sugar; beat until smooth and thick. Remove from the heat, add the butter, and cool. Fold in the whipped cream and fruits. Pour into 6x10x2-inch dish and chill 24 hours. Slice and serve on crisp lettuce leaves.   *8 servings.*

GREEN GODDESS SALAD

A classic salad that originated in California. Wasn't there a movie called "Green Goddess"?

¾ cup mayonnaise
½ cup sour cream
2 tablespoons finely chopped green
   onion
¼ cup finely chopped parsley
1 teaspoon dried tarragon leaves
1 tablespoon tarragon vinegar
1 tablespoon anchovy paste
1 clove garlic, minced
1 head romaine lettuce
1 head Boston lettuce

Soak the tarragon leaves in vinegar for 5 to 10 minutes, then strain. Stir the vinegar into the mayonnaise, discarding the tarragon leaves. Add all the other ingredients except lettuce. Mix well. Chill for 1 hour.

To serve, break romaine and Boston lettuce into bite-size pieces in a salad bowl. Toss with the chilled dressing to coat the greens well.   *6 servings.*

SPINACH SALAD

Our favorite salad and our very favorite way to enjoy spinach. But then, we're partial to the stuff.

1 pound fresh spinach
2 hard-cooked eggs, cut into wedges
1 large ripe tomato, cut into wedges
½ red onion, thinly sliced
½ teaspoon salt
1 clove garlic, halved
4 slices bacon, crisply fried and
   crumbled

Wash the spinach, remove stems and tear leaves into bite-size pieces. Dry thoroughly and chill for 2 hours.

Just before serving, sprinkle the salt in a salad bowl and rub the bowl with garlic halves. Add all the other ingredients and toss with Golden Salad Dressing. See page 63. *4 servings.*

BLOODY MARY SALAD

A piquant variation of the Creamy Tomato Aspic on page 59.

4 cups tomato-vegetable juice
2 3-ounce packages of lemon gelatin
1½ teaspoons Worcestershire sauce
½ teaspoon salt
⅛ teaspoon pepper
¾ cup crumbled blue cheese
⅓ cup minced onion
1 tablespoon lime juice

Bring the juice to a boil. Dissolve the gelatin in the hot juice. Stir in Worcestershire sauce, salt and pepper. Chill until slightly thickened. Fold in the blue cheese, onion and lime juice. Pour into a 1½-quart mold. Chill until firm. *6-8 servings.*

CREAMY TOMATO ASPIC

An ideal summer luncheon dish with slices of cold meat.

1 envelope unflavored gelatin
¼ cup water
1 8-ounce can tomato sauce
1 tablespoon lime juice
½ cup sour cream
¼ cup Chablis wine
¼ teaspoon salt
2 tablespoons minced onion
2 teaspoons minced fresh parsley
½ cup celery, chopped fine

Soften the gelatin in the water. Heat the tomato sauce to boiling, then dissolve the gelatin in it. Stir in all the ingredients except the celery. Chill until the mixture thickens, then fold in the celery. Turn into a 1-quart mold and chill until firm, about 4 hours.   *4 servings.*

JELLIED TOMATO SHRIMP SALAD

A main-course luncheon dish.

>2 envelopes unflavored gelatin
>½ cup cold water
>1 cup boiling water
>1 15-ounce can tomato sauce
>1 tablespoon lemon juice
>1 tablespoon Worcestershire sauce
>1 teaspoon salt
>⅛ teaspoon white pepper
>1 cup sour cream
>1½ cups cooked shrimp, cut up
>2 hard-cooked eggs, diced
>½ cup minced celery
>⅓ cup sliced, pimiento-stuffed green
>   olives

Sprinkle the gelatin over the cold water to soften for about 5 minutes; add the boiling water and stir until the gelatin dissolves. Stir in the tomato sauce, lemon juice, Worcestershire sauce, salt and pepper. Cool.

Add the sour cream and beat until combined. Chill until slightly thickened and fold in the remaining ingredients.

Pour into six individual molds and serve on crisp salad greens garnished with sliced cucumbers and lemon wedges. *6 servings.*

TUNA GARDEN SALAD

When company comes and the budget will allow it, substitute shrimp or crabmeat for the tuna.

>2 envelopes unflavored gelatin
>¾ cup cold water
>1 can condensed cream of chicken soup
>1 cup mayonnaise

2 tablespoons lemon juice
1 tablespoon prepared mustard
1½ cups tuna, drained and flaked
½ cup chopped celery
½ cup chopped cucumber
¼ cup chopped green pepper

Soften the gelatin in cold water. Heat the soup to boiling and add the gelatin, stirring to dissolve. Stir in the mayonnaise, lemon juice and mustard. Chill until partially set; fold in the tuna, celery, cucumber and green pepper. Turn into an 8½x4½x2½-inch loaf pan. Chill until firm.

To serve, slice and place on shredded lettuce. Garnish with pitted ripe olives. *8 servings.*

AVOCADO DRESSING

Use this on a chef's salad for an elegant taste and color combination.

1 large ripe avocado
½ teaspoon salt
1 teaspoon lemon juice
2 tablespoons tomato sauce
2 tablespoons chopped sweet red onion
¼ teaspoon Tabasco sauce
2 tablespoons chopped fresh parsley
2 tablespoons salad oil
1 tablespoon cider vinegar

Peel the avocado, remove pit and chop the meat into small pieces. Add the other ingredients, folding together to mix thoroughly.

Makes enough for 8 individual chef's salads.

BLUE CHEESE DRESSING

This full-bodied dressing is made quickly in the blender.

¾ cup salad oil
⅓ cup buttermilk
¼ cup vinegar
2 tablespoons mayonnaise
1 teaspoon salt
½ teaspoon dry mustard
⅛ teaspoon garlic powder
4 tablespoons blue cheese

Put all the ingredients in the blender container. Blend on high speed for 5 seconds.   *Makes 1½ cups.*

CELERY SEED DRESSING

Good with fruit salads.

1 teaspoon grated onion
½ teaspoon salt
½ teaspoon dry mustard
½ teaspoon paprika
½ teaspoon celery seed
½ cup salad oil
2 tablespoons honey
3 tablespoons vinegar

Combine all the ingredients in a jar with a tight-fitting lid and shake until well blended.   *Makes ¾ cup.*

COLE SLAW DRESSING

Don't take the easy way out — with mayonnaise alone. Your *slaw deserves something special — and this is it.*

½ cup mayonnaise
1 cup sour cream

4 tablespoons wine vinegar
4 tablespoons sugar
1 teaspoon salt
¼ teaspoon pepper

Mix the mayonnaise and sour cream together. Add — and stir constantly while you're doing it — the wine vinegar, sugar, salt and pepper. *Makes 2 cups.*

FRUIT SALAD DRESSING

Almost everybody seems to like this one.

1 8-ounce package cream cheese
1½ cups orange juice
3 tablespoons lemon juice
1 teaspoon salt
3 tablespoons sugar
1 teaspoon paprika
2 teaspoons celery seed

Soften the cream cheese and blend well with the other ingredients. *Makes 2½ cups.*

GOLDEN SALAD DRESSING

Why buy a salad dressing mix or a prepared dressing when such a good one is so easy to make?

¼ cup sugar
¼ cup prepared mustard
¼ cup tarragon vinegar
¼ cup sherry
2 teaspoons salt
¾ cup salad oil
½ teaspoon Worcestershire sauce

Put all the ingredients together in a jar with a tight-fitting top and shake well. *Makes 2 cups.*

LOW CALORIE DRESSING

A good dressing for the not-so-slim. But non-dieters like it, too.

⅓ cup water
1 beef bouillon cube
½ cup wine vinegar
⅓ cup tomato juice
2 teaspoons honey
1 teaspoon instant minced onion
1 teaspoon finely chopped parsley

Dissolve the bouillon cube in the boiling water. Cool. Add the other ingredients and shake hard to blend.
Makes 1¾ cups.

PIQUANT DRESSING

Has a lot more character than the average dressing.

½ cup salad oil
3 tablespoons cider vinegar
1 teaspoon salt
⅛ teaspoon pepper
¼ teaspoon paprika
1 teaspoon sugar
1 tablespoon chopped green pepper
1 tablespoon chopped sweet red pepper
1 teaspoon finely chopped parsley
1 teaspoon finely chopped chives
1 tablespoon chopped sweet red onion

Combine all the ingredients and chill. Shake well before serving. *Makes 1 cup.*

SALAD DRESSING MIX

Handy to have on hand when you need to make a dressing in a hurry.

4 teaspoons salt
1 teaspoon dried minced garlic
4 teaspoons instant minced onion
1 teaspoon black pepper
1 teaspoon sugar
1 teaspoon paprika

Combine the ingredients and store, tightly covered, in a cool, dry place.

To use, combine ¼ cup vinegar with 1½ teaspoons of the above mix and ⅔ cup salad oil. Shake well.

Enough mix for 8 cups liquid.

BOILED SALAD DRESSING

A little trouble to make but you can taste the difference.

2 tablespoons flour
1½ tablespoons sugar
1½ teaspoons dry mustard
1 teaspoon salt
3 egg yolks
½ cup evaporated milk
¼ cup light cream
½ cup cider vinegar
2 tablespoons butter

Mix together the flour, sugar, mustard, salt and egg yolks. Add the evaporated milk; mix well and turn into a double boiler. Cook over boiling water, stirring constantly, until the mixture is heated through. Add the cream and vinegar alternately, a few drops at a time. Stir and beat the mixture while it cooks, until thick and smooth. Remove from the stove, and stir in the butter. When the butter is melted, strain the dressing.

Makes 1¾ cups.

UNCOOKED SALAD DRESSING

You can add chutney, curry, chopped cucumber or chopped egg to this.

 2 eggs, beaten
 1 teaspoon salt
 1 teaspoon mustard
 1 14-ounce can sweetened condensed
   milk
 1 cup vinegar

Beat the eggs, salt, mustard and milk vigorously for a few minutes. Add the vinegar, stir well and set aside for 3 or 4 hours to thicken.   *Makes 3 cups.*

SWEET AND SOUR DRESSING

If your family needs a little encouragement to eat salads, this will help.

 ½ cup olive oil
 ½ cup cider vinegar
 ¼ cup sugar
 2 tablespoons minced onions
 2 tablespoons minced celery
 1 tablespoon minced green pepper
 1 teaspoon dry mustard
 1 teaspoon Worcestershire sauce
 1 teaspoon salt
 ⅛ teaspoon pepper

Combine all the ingredients and shake well.
                    Makes 1½ cups.

VINAIGRETTE SAUCE

Use it on jellied meats and poultry as well as salads.

 ½ cup olive oil
 3 tablespoons vinegar or lemon juice
 ¾ teaspoon salt

1 clove garlic, minced
⅛ teaspoon pepper
⅛ teaspoon paprika
¼ teaspoon dry mustard
1 teaspoon Worcestershire sauce

Here again, all you do is place the ingredients in a jar and shake it up! *Makes about ¾ cup.*

YOGURT DRESSING

Try this on paper-thin slices of cucumber and onion.

1 cup plain yogurt
¼ cup sliced green onion
1 clove garlic, minced
1 teaspoon dried mint
1 tablespoon lemon juice
½ teaspoon salt
⅛ teaspoon white pepper

Combine thoroughly and chill.

Makes enough to dress 4 cups of cucumber and onion slices.

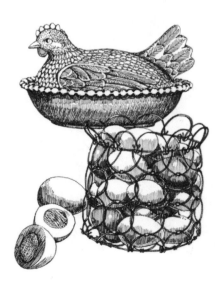

MAIN COURSE DISHES
-or-
Nothing ventured,
nothing gained

Most of us have favorite foods, and a few of us have un-favorites which we won't touch simply because we dislike them or they disagree with us. But don't you hate it when people turn up their noses at perfectly fine fare just because they never had it before or don't even know what it is? Bad enough when *kids* do it!

Same with recipes. Some people often hesitate to try a new or different recipe just because it has a fancy name and they think it's difficult to make. Nonsense. Some of the most impressive-sounding dishes are easiest to put together. If you've ever made ham and eggs, you shouldn't have any trouble with Eggs Benedict. All it takes to turn scrambled eggs into an omelet is a little more tender loving care. Crêpes Suzette are thin pancakes. Boeuf Bourguignon is stew. Baked Alaska is ice cream pie.

By the same token, just because a dish has a foreign title and a dashing air, it doesn't follow that the dish is great. Steak Tartare is raw meat, and you can have it.

All of which serves to introduce our chapter on MAIN COURSE DISHES, every one of which we're sure you and your guests will enjoy. *"Bon appétit"* as the gourmets say.

GROUND BEEF CABBAGE CASSEROLE

An easier-to-make version of the conventional stuffed cabbage roll. It tastes just as good, and, for some reason, youngsters seem to like it better.

1 medium onion, chopped
6 tablespoons butter or margarine, divided
1 pound ground chuck
1 cup cooked rice
1 small cabbage
2 tablespoons flour
2 cloves garlic, minced
2 tablespoons catsup
1 cup canned tomatoes
1 cup water
2 tablespoons chopped parsley
1½ teaspoons salt
¼ teaspoon pepper

Sauté the onion in 2 tablespoons butter or margarine until soft. Add the beef and rice and cook briskly for about 3 minutes, stirring. Turn into a shallow casserole, about 2½-quart size. Shred cabbage finely and arrange over the meat mixture.

Melt the remaining 4 tablespoons butter or margarine and blend in the flour. Cook until bubbly, then remove from the heat and stir in the garlic, catsup, tomatoes, water, parsley, salt and pepper. Simmer, stirring, about 5 minutes. Pour over cabbage. Cover and bake at 350°F for 30 minutes. *Serves 6-8.*

ORIENTAL BEEF AND PEPPERS

When you feel like showing off right at the table in front of your guests, here's a good dish to do it with. Use an electric frying pan, chafing dish or wok. Ahhh so!

1 tablespoon cornstarch
¼ cup cold water
3 pounds beef, cut into thin strips (top round or sirloin)
3 cloves garlic, minced
1 teaspoon powdered ginger
¾ cup corn or peanut oil
2 tomatoes, peeled and cut into small wedges
2 green peppers, seeded and cut into julienne strips
2 onions, finely chopped
1 can consommé or beef bouillon
1 teaspoon sugar
1 teaspoon salt
1 tablespoon soy sauce
¼ cup dry sherry

Mix the cornstarch and water into a smooth paste. Combine this mixture with the beef strips, garlic and ginger. Heat oil in a heavy skillet and add the meat mixture. Cook for 5 minutes over high heat, stirring constantly. Remove the meat, but leave the oil in the skillet. Reduce the heat to medium and cook the tomatoes, green peppers and onions in the hot oil for 2 minutes. (Vegetables must be crisp.)

Add the consommé or bouillon, sugar, salt, soy sauce and sherry, stirring constantly. Cook for 3 minutes. Add the meat and cook about 2 minutes, or until heated through. Serve immediately, with steamed rice. *Serves 8.*

RED FLANNEL HASH

The next time you have roast beef or corned beef, make sure there's enough left over to make Red Flannel Hash.

> 2 cups chopped, cooked roast beef or
>   corned beef
> 2 cups chopped, cooked potatoes
> 2 cups chopped, cooked beets
> ¼ cup finely chopped onion
> 1 garlic clove, minced
> 1 teaspoon salt
> ¼ teaspoon pepper
> ¼ teaspoon dry mustard
> 6 slices bacon
> ½ cup light cream

Thoroughly combine all ingredients except the bacon and the cream. Place in a 9-inch square baking pan. Arrange bacon slices on top. Cover with the cream. Bake in a 350°F oven for 45 minutes.   *Serves 6.*

LASAGNE

Make it now, bake it later. Add a tossed green salad and you have a complete meal.

> ½ pound lasagne noodles
> 4 quarts boiling water
> 1 tablespoon salt
> 1 tablespoon salad oil
> 1 quart meat sauce (see page 73)
> ¾ pound mozzarella cheese
> ¾ pound ricotta cheese
> 3 tablespoons grated Parmesan cheese

Cook the noodles in boiling water with salt and oil for 10 minutes or until "chewy" but not soft. Drain.

Cover the bottom of a 9x12-inch baking dish with ⅓ of meat sauce. Layer one third of the mozzarella sliced thin over the sauce and top that with one third of the ricotta. Add a layer of cooked noodles.

Repeat the above sequence using the remaining ingredients, ending with a layer of meat sauce. Sprinkle with grated Parmesan.

Bake in a 375°F oven for 25 minutes, or until the mozzarella is melted and the Parmesan is brown.

Serves 6.

MEAT SAUCE

Sure you can buy good meat sauce. But homemade is better — and less expensive.

3 tablespoons olive oil
1 cup onion, chopped
½ cup celery, chopped
1 clove garlic, minced
½ pound ground beef
½ pound bulk pork sausage
1 teaspoon salt
⅛ teaspoon black pepper
½ cup tomato juice
¼ teaspoon dry red pepper
3 ounces tomato paste
2 cups canned tomatoes
¼ teaspoon oregano
¼ teaspoon basil

Sauté the onion, celery and garlic in olive oil for about 5 minutes. Remove the vegetables and brown the beef and sausage meat in the remaining oil. Combine the meat and vegetables in a 3-quart saucepan, add remaining ingredients, and simmer for 1½ hours. Serve over cooked spaghetti. This is also the sauce we use in our Lasagne recipe on page 72. *Makes 1 quart.*

SPICED MEAT LOAF

If meat loaf ever becomes a "company" dish, this is the one that will make it.

    1 pound ground chuck
    ½ pound ground veal
    ½ pound ground pork
    1 medium onion, grated
    1 egg, beaten
    1 cup soft bread crumbs
    ½ cup milk
    1 teaspoon salt
    ¼ teaspoon pepper
    ½ teaspoon nutmeg
    ½ teaspoon allspice
    ⅛ teaspoon ginger

Combine all ingredients, but *lightly*. Shape into a loaf and bake in a 9x5x2¾-inch pan at 350°F for 1¼ hours.

Serves 6.

ITALIAN MEATBALLS

Not too spicy, not too bland — just right. Please handle gently as you form into balls.

    ¾ pound ground beef
    ¼ pound bulk pork sausage
    1 cup dry bread crumbs
    ½ cup grated Parmesan cheese
    1 tablespoon fresh parsley, chopped
    1 clove garlic, minced
    ½ cup milk
    1 teaspoon salt
    ¼ teaspoon pepper
    2 beaten eggs
    2 tablespoons olive oil

Mix all the ingredients except the oil and form into balls, handling as gently as possible. Brown in the olive oil. Cover with Tomato Sauce (see below) and simmer for 25 minutes. Serve with spaghetti.

Serves 4.

TOMATO SAUCE

3 tablespoons olive oil
1 large Bermuda onion, chopped
2 stalks celery, chopped
½ green pepper, chopped
1 clove garlic, minced
4 cups canned, peeled tomatoes
½ teaspoon thyme
1 teaspoon salt
⅛ teaspoon pepper
1 teaspoon sugar
½ cup water

Sauté the onion, celery, green pepper and garlic in the oil for 5 minutes. Add the other ingredients and cook gently for 20 minutes. Pour the sauce over the meatballs and simmer for another 25 minutes before serving.

SWEET-SOUR MEATBALLS

An all-American dish with a Chinese accent.

1 pound ground chuck
1 teaspoon salt
1 tablespoon minced onion
¼ cup fine dry bread crumbs
1 egg, slightly beaten
1 1-pound can pineapple chunks,
    drained (reserve ⅓ cup of syrup)
⅔ cup catsup
⅔ cup cider vinegar
⅓ cup light brown sugar, packed

Mix the beef, salt, onion, crumbs, egg, reserved pineapple syrup and ½ cup of the chunks, cut very small. Shape into small balls.

Bring the catsup, vinegar and brown sugar to a boil. Add the meatballs and remaining pineapple chunks. Simmer, covered for 25 minutes. Serve hot, with cooked rice. *Makes 40 to 50 meatballs.*

CHILI CON CARNE

The green tomatoes give this chili extra character.

> 6 medium onions, chopped
> 4 garlic cloves, minced
> 3 tablespoons bacon fat
> 1½ pounds ground chuck
> 1 #2½ can red kidney beans
> 3 tablespoons sugar
> 3 tablespoons vinegar
> 3 tablespoons chili powder
> 10 medium green tomatoes, peeled and
> coarsely cut
> 1 cup water

Sauté the onions and garlic in bacon fat. Remove the vegetables, then brown the meat in same skillet. Place the meat, onions and garlic in a covered earthenware pot or casserole and mix in the rest of the ingredients.

Cook in a 300°F oven for 4 hours. If the chili seems too thin, remove the cover and let the chili cook down until thicker. *Serves 6-8.*

BRAISED LAMB SHANKS

A big, hearty dish, perfect when you know everybody has the hungries.

> 6 1-pound lamb shanks
> 1 clove garlic
> 3 tablespoons vegetable oil
> 1 onion, chopped
> 1½ cups beef bouillon or stock
> ¼ cup lemon juice
> 1½ teaspoons salt
> ¼ teaspoon pepper
> 1 bay leaf

Rub the lamb shanks with the garlic clove and brown in oil. Remove from the pan. Sauté the chopped onion in the oil. Place the shanks and onion in a covered oven casserole and add the other ingredients, mixed together. Bake in a 325°F oven for 1½ hours, or until the lamb is tender.

Strain the stock and skim off the fat. Serve the shanks with the stock in dinner-size flat soup bowls, with new potatoes sprinkled with fresh chopped parsley. *Serves 6.*

BARBECUED POT ROAST

All pot roasts are not created equal. This one has a sauce that makes it better.

    4- to 5-pound beef pot roast
    2 teaspoons salt
    ¼ teaspoon pepper
    2 tablespoons butter or margarine
    ½ cup water
    1 cup tomato juice
    3 medium onions, chopped
    3 cloves garlic, sliced
    2 tablespoons brown sugar
    ½ teaspoon dry mustard
    ¼ cup lemon juice
    ¼ cup vinegar
    ¼ cup catsup
    1 tablespoon Worcestershire sauce

Rub the surface of the roast with salt and pepper. Brown in butter or margarine on all sides. Add the water, tomato juice, chopped onions, and sliced garlic. Simmer for 1½ hours. Mix the remaining ingredients, add to the meat and simmer for 2 hours.

The gravy may be strained before serving, but it is very good just the way it is. *Serves 8-10.*

BEEFSTEAK AND KIDNEY PIE

Here's the best recipe we've ever found for this classic English dish.

> 1 pound round steak, cut into 1-inch cubes
> 1 pound beef kidneys
> 1½ teaspoons salt
> ½ teaspoon pepper
> 2 tablespoons flour
> 3 tablespoons butter or margarine
> 2 tablespoons flour
> 1 cup chopped onion
> 2½ cups beef stock
> ¼ cup water

Parboil the kidneys for 2 minutes. Remove the membrane and cut into 1-inch cubes. Mix salt and pepper with 2 tablespoons flour and sprinkle over the steak. Brown the steak cubes in butter. Add the onion, kidney and beef stock. (Beef stock can be made by adding 3 bouillon cubes to 2½ cups water.)

Simmer for 1¼ hours, or until the meat is tender. Thicken stock with the remaining 2 tablespoons flour blended with ¼ cup water.

Place the meat mixture in a 2-quart casserole. Cover the top with Special Meat Pie Pastry (below), and make a hole in the center of the crust in order that the steam may escape. Bake in a 400°F oven for 12 to 15 minutes, or until golden brown.   *Serves 6.*

SPECIAL MEAT PIE PASTRY

Use also for Canadian Pork Pie (page 82), Quiche Lorraine (page 86), and Veal and Ham Pie (page 87).

> 4 cups all-purpose flour
> ½ teaspoon salt
> 1 cup lard

⅓ cup butter
3 tablespoons milk
2 tablespoons water
2 eggs

Sift the flour and salt together. Cut in one half of the lard until pieces are the size of peas.

Bring the remaining lard, butter, milk and water to a boil. With a wooden spoon, stir half the hot mixture into the flour. Then blend in one egg, beaten, and the remaining hot mixture. Handling lightly, knead until smooth. Let stand 10 minutes to cool slightly.

Roll on a lightly floured board to ¼-inch thickness. Beat the remaining egg and brush over the top of the pie before baking.

Makes a 9-inch 2-crust pie.

BEEF STROGANOFF

A classic — and very easy to prepare. A filet is the best cut of beef to use. Flank is cheaper and has equally good flavor, but it's coarser and not quite as tender.

     2 pounds beef filet or flank
     4 tablespoons butter or margarine,
        divided
     1 onion, minced
     ½ pound fresh mushrooms, sliced
     2 tablespoons flour
     2 cups beef stock or bouillon
     ½ teaspoon paprika
     ½ teaspoon salt
     ¼ teaspoon freshly ground pepper
     1 cup sour cream

Cut the beef into little slivers about 1 inch long, ½ inch wide and ¼ inch thick. Brown in 2 tablespoons butter or margarine for about 5 minutes. Remove from pan and keep hot. Sauté the minced onion for about 2 minutes and add to the browned meat.

Add remaining 2 tablespoons butter or margarine to the pan and sauté the mushrooms. Remove the mushrooms and place with the beef. Add the flour to the pan; brown for 3 minutes. Add to the pan the stock, paprika, salt and pepper. When the sauce has thickened, add the sour cream, which should be at room temperature. Heat through gently. Pour the sauce over the meat, onions and mushrooms and sprinkle with additional paprika. Serve with noodles.   *Serves 4-6.*

LONDON BROIL

One of the most flavorful of all steak dishes and one of the most inexpensive if you carve it right: across the grain, paper-thin, with the knife almost parallel to the cutting board. So while you start with a piece of meat that's only about one inch thick, each slice is about 2 inches wide. (That's where the

*economy comes in; a little looks like a lot.) There's absolutely
no waste, either.*

> 1 beef flank steak, 1½ to 2 pounds
> ½ cup salad oil
> ¼ cup vinegar or red Burgundy wine
> ¼ cup soy sauce
> 2 teaspoons Worcestershire sauce
> 1 bay leaf
> ⅛ teaspoon pepper
> ⅛ teaspoon ground cloves
> dash cayenne pepper

Score the surface of the steak on both sides. Combine all the other ingredients for a marinade. Place the meat in a flat utility dish and pour the marinade over it. Cover and refrigerate for 12 hours, turning occasionally. Remove from the marinade.

Preheat broiler. Broil steak 2 to 3 inches below heat, about 5 minutes on each side. A flank should be cooked rare or it will toughen. Serve with the classic Béarnaise Sauce (see below).   *Serves 4.*

BEARNAISE SAUCE

A classic sauce.

> ½ cup Burgundy wine
> 2 tablespoons tarragon vinegar
> 1 tablespoon finely chopped onion
> ⅛ teaspoon pepper
> ½ teaspoon dried tarragon leaves
> ¼ teaspoon dried chervil leaves
> 3 egg yolks, beaten
> ¾ cup melted butter

Combine the wine, vinegar, onion, pepper, tarragon and chervil in top of double boiler. Cook over direct heat until reduced by half. Strain the mixture. Allow to cool.

Beating briskly over hot water, add alternately, a little at a time, the egg yolks and melted butter. When finished the sauce will have the consistency of Hollandaise Sauce.

Makes 1½ cups.

CANADIAN PORK PIE

This recipe came right out of French Canada, and we've never tasted a better one. Makes a particularly good luncheon or late supper dish.

    2 tablespoons butter or margarine
    1 onion, finely minced
    1 pound lean ground pork
    1 pound lean ground veal
    1 teaspoon salt
    ½ teaspoon pepper
    ½ teaspoon thyme
    ½ teaspoon nutmeg
    ¼ teaspoon sage
    ⅛ teaspoon allspice
      Special Meat Pie Pastry for 2-crust pie
        (page 78)

Sauté the onion in butter or margarine in a heavy frying pan. Combine the pork, veal, salt, pepper, thyme, nutmeg, sage and allspice. Add the seasoned meat to the sautéed onion and cook slowly for 20 minutes, stirring to prevent sticking. Strain off any excess fat and cool the mixture.

Line a 9-inch pie plate with half of the pastry. Fill with the cooked meat mixture. Top with the remaining pastry. Crimp the edges and seal carefully. Slash the top to permit steam to escape.

Bake in a 400°F oven for about 15 minutes. Lower the heat to 350°F and bake 20 minutes more, or until nicely browned.   *Serves 6.*

GLAZED TWIN LOINS OF PORK

The perfect dish for that special sit-down dinner party. Go all out and have it carved at the table.

    2 loins of pork, 4 to 5 pounds each,
      boned
    2½ cups cooked rice

> 1 teaspoon curry powder
> ½ cup chopped onion
> 2 tablespoons butter or margarine
> 3 tablespoons minced parsley

Sauté the onion in butter or margarine until golden. Add the rice, curry powder and parsley, mixing well. Allow to cool.

Sprinkle one loin of pork, fat side down, with a little salt and pepper. Spoon the rice mixture on top, keeping the layer as level as possible. Place the other loin, fat side up, on top. Tie the two loins together about every 2 inches. Place on a rack in the roasting pan. Roast at 350°F, allowing 35 minutes to the pound.

GLAZE

Forty minutes before roast is done, pour off the pan drippings, remove the rack and put the pork directly in the pan. Pour over one third of glaze (see below) and roast 20 minutes. Add one third more of the glaze and roast for the last 20 minutes. Baste occasionally. Heat the remaining glaze with remaining ½ cup of bouillon and pass when roast is served.

> 1 8-ounce can tomato sauce
> ½ cup catsup
> ½ cup vinegar
> ⅓ cup honey
> ½ cup light corn syrup
> 1 cup beef bouillon
> 1 tablespoon cornstarch
> 4 tablespoons Grand Marnier liqueur

Combine the tomato sauce, catsup, vinegar, honey, corn syrup and half of the bouillon. Bring to a boil and simmer for about 5 minutes. Mix the cornstarch with a little water and stir into the first mixture. Cook until thickened. Add the liqueur and simmer for 10 minutes before using.   *Serves 8-10.*

ORANGE PORK CHOPS

If there's one food item that needs jazzing up, it's a pork chop. And while there doesn't seem to be anything special about this recipe on paper, the finished product is exceptionally good.

> 4 thick pork chops
> 1 clove garlic
> grated rind of 1 orange
> 1 cup orange juice
> 1 cup sour cream

Rub the pork chops with the garlic clove. Trim off the fat and rub it over the inside of the frying pan. Brown the meat.

Place in a covered casserole with the orange rind and juice and bake in a 350°F oven for 1 hour.

Before serving, add the sour cream, which has been brought to room temperature, to the juices in the casserole. This goes well with Oven Baked Rice. (See recipe on page 136.)   *Serves 4.*

HAM DIVAN

A particularly good luncheon dish which can be prepared in advance. Most of your guests will appreciate the trouble you took to make it.

> 2 pounds fresh asparagus
> 4 tablespoons butter
> 4 tablespoons flour
> 2 cups milk
> ½ teaspoon salt
> ½ cup whipped cream
> 2 teaspoons grated lemon rind
> 6 thin slices of cooked ham
> ¼ cup Parmesan cheese

Break or cut off the tough stalk ends of the asparagus. Remove the scales and wash off any sand which may have collected under them. Arrange the stalks in a shallow pan and cover with water and 1 teaspoon salt. Bring to a boil and cook for 6 to 8 minutes, or until tender but still crisp. Lift out carefully with a slotted spoon or tongs; arrange into six bundles.

Make a sauce by stirring the flour into the butter until it bubbles. Add the milk and salt and stir until thickened. Fold in the whipped cream and lemon rind.

Roll a ham slice around each of the asparagus bundles and place in a baking dish. Pour sauce over all and sprinkle with Parmesan cheese.

Bake in a 375°F oven for 15 minutes. Then slide under pre-heated broiler for 2 or 3 minutes, or until lightly browned. *Serves 6.*

HAM STEAK WITH CIDER SAUCE

Here's a good example of how a good sauce can turn an ordinary dish into something uncommonly good.

1 ham steak, 1½ inches thick
1 teaspoon dry mustard
¼ cup apple jelly
¾ cup apple cider
1 tablespoon cornstarch
2 tablespoons cold water
¼ teaspoon grated lemon rind
1 cup seedless green grapes, halved

Rub the ham steak on both sides with mustard and place in a shallow baking dish. Bake 30 minutes in a 350°F oven.

Heat the jelly and cider together and pour over the steak. Bake an additional 30 minutes, basting frequently.

Remove the ham to a warm platter. Mix the cornstarch with the water. Stir in the liquids from the baking dish and heat to boiling, stirring all the while. Simmer one minute. Add the lemon rind and grapes and reheat. Serve over the ham. *Serves 4.*

QUICHE LORRAINE

One of the greatest lunch or brunch dishes ever invented. Prepare in advance, freeze, and bake when needed. All you need to complete the meal is a nice tossed salad.

1½ cups grated natural Swiss cheese
4 tablespoons flour
½ cup finely chopped cooked ham
3 eggs
1 cup milk
¼ teaspoon salt
¼ teaspoon dry mustard
1 9-inch unbaked pie shell (see Special Meat Pie Pastry recipe on page 78)

Combine the cheese and flour and sprinkle into the pie shell. Spread the ham evenly over this. Combine the eggs, milk, salt and mustard. Beat until smooth and pour evenly over the cheese and ham.

Bake at 375° for 45 minutes, or until the custard is set. Serve warm, garnished with chopped parsley.   *Serves 6.*

VEAL AND HAM PIE

A popular dish in the better London pubs. Should be served cold and if you can find some English ale to go along with it, so much the better.

> 2 pounds lean stewing veal
> ½ pound cooked ham
> 1 teaspoon rosemary
> 1½ teaspoons salt
> ½ teaspoon freshly ground black pepper
> 2 hard-cooked eggs
> Special Meat Pie Pastry for 2-crust pie
>   (page 78)

Prepare the pastry and line with it a 9x5x3-inch loaf pan, including the sides. Put the veal and ham through the coarse blade of a meat grinder. Mix with the rosemary, salt and pepper. Place half the meat mixture in the loaf pan.

Halve the shelled eggs lengthwise. Place face down along the length of the pan and cover with the remaining meat mixture. Top with the remaining pastry, making slits in the pastry to allow the steam to escape. Bake 10 minutes in a 425°F oven.

Reduce the oven temperature to 325°F. Brush the top of the pie with beaten egg reserved from the pastry recipe and bake about 2½ hours longer. If you can see a hollow through a center slit in the pie, fill with ½ envelope unflavored gelatin dissolved in 1 cup chicken broth.

Cool the pie, remove from pan and refrigerate. Slice and serve cold.   *Serves 8.*

VEAL PARMIGIANA

The veal must be pounded thin in Parmigiana, just as it is in Piccata, if you're aiming for perfection. Do all the preparation in advance and bake after your guests arrive.

THE SAUCE SAVORY

    3 finely minced, peeled cloves garlic
    1 onion, minced
    3 tablespoons olive oil
    2½ cups canned tomatoes
    1¼ teaspoons salt
    ¼ teaspoon pepper
    1 8-ounce can tomato sauce
    ¼ teaspoon oregano

In a saucepan, sauté the garlic and onion in hot oil until golden. Add the tomatoes, salt, and pepper. Break up the tomatoes; simmer uncovered for 10 minutes. Add the tomato sauce and oregano. Simmer 20 minutes.

THE VEAL

    1 pound veal cutlets, pounded thin
    1 egg, beaten
    1 cup fine bread crumbs
    ¼ cup grated Parmesan cheese
    3 tablespoons olive oil

Dip each piece of veal first in egg, then in a mixture of crumbs and Parmesan. Sauté two or three pieces at a time in 1 tablespoon hot oil in a skillet. When browned on the bottom, loosen the crumbs from the skillet and turn with a broad spatula. Sauté until golden brown underneath. Set the veal slices side-by-side in a 13x9x2-inch baking dish. Repeat with the rest of the veal.

PUTTING IT ALL TOGETHER

½ pound mozzarella or Muenster cheese
⅓ cup grated Parmesan cheese

Slice the cheese thinly. Pour ⅔ of the tomato sauce over the veal, straining the sauce if desired. Arrange the cheese slices on top. Spoon on the rest of the sauce. Sprinkle with Parmesan. Bake at 350°F for 30 minutes.

Serves 4.

VEAL PICCATA

Next time you entertain a true gourmet, demonstrate your knowledge of good food by serving Veal Piccata. But make sure you pound the meat paper thin — that's the secret of its delicate flavor and texture.

1½ pounds veal cutlets
½ cup lemon juice
1 tablespoon flour
4 tablespoons butter or margarine
1 tablespoon chopped parsley
⅛ teaspoon pepper

Pound the cutlets until slices are flat and paper thin. (Use your fist or a wooden mallet.) Dredge lightly with flour. Heat the butter or margarine in a frying pan until bubbling and sauté each cutlet on both sides for about 3 minutes. Remove from the pan and keep warm.

Deglaze the pan with lemon juice, heat to boiling and pour over the cutlets. Sprinkle with chopped parsley and pepper.

Serves 4.

VEAL SCALLOPINE MARSALA

A dish you'll find only in the best restaurants. And when you do, this is how it's prepared.

1½ pounds veal, trimmed and boneless
3 tablespoons flour
½ pound fresh mushrooms, thinly sliced
¼ cup butter or margarine
¼ cup veal or chicken stock
¼ cup Marsala wine
1 tablespoon lemon juice
lemon slices
parsley

Sauté the mushrooms in the butter or margarine. Remove the mushrooms with a slotted spoon; set aside and keep warm.

Pound the veal slices very thin, then dredge lightly with flour on one side only. Sauté in the butter, floured-side down. When the juices show on the upper side, turn the meat and sauté until brown. Remove from the pan and keep warm.

Add the stock, wine, and lemon juice to the pan juices. Heat to the simmering point and pour over mushroom-topped veal slices. Garnish with a lemon slice and fresh chopped parsley. *Serves 4.*

SAVORY LIVER LOAF

People who swore they wouldn't eat liver in any *form have tried this and liked it. Serve it hot or cold; mixed with chopped pickles; on crackers, with cocktails.*

1 pound beef liver, sliced and skinned
1 egg
2 tablespoons tomato catsup
1 small onion, chopped
1 clove garlic
1½ teaspoons salt

¼ teaspoon pepper
1 pound pork sausage meat
½ cup toasted wheat germ

Put the egg and catsup in the blender. Cut the liver in small chunks and add gradually, with the chopped onion, to the egg mixture. Add the garlic, salt, and pepper. Blend until the entire mixture is smooth.

Transfer to a large bowl and add the sausage meat and wheat germ. Spread in a greased 9x5x3-inch loaf pan and bake at 325°F for 1 hour. *Serves 6.*

BEEF TONGUE WITH TANGY SAUCE

Tongue is very nutritious and still relatively economical. Dressed up in this Tangy Sauce you can serve it to anybody. And they'll like it.

2½ to 3 pounds fresh beef tongue
2 onions, chopped
2 stalks celery, diced
8 peppercorns
4 whole cloves
6 sprigs parsley

Put all the ingredients in a pot with boiling water to cover and simmer for 3 hours. Remove the tongue and skin it; take out the roots and gristle. To serve hot, return briefly to the cooking liquid and reheat. Slice thinly and serve with Tangy Sauce (see below). *Serves 6-8.*

TANGY SAUCE

1 cup red currant or blackberry jelly
2 tablespoons prepared mustard
2 tablespoons vinegar
¼ teaspoon powdered cloves
½ teaspoon cinnamon

Melt the jelly over hot water and stir in the other ingredients. Serve hot.

LAMB KIDNEY STEW

You'll have to keep this treat for people you know like kidneys. Highly nutritious and relatively inexpensive. The flavor is superb if you're careful to cook the kidneys lightly.

1 pound lamb kidneys
3 tablespoons butter or margarine
1 medium onion, chopped
2 tablespoons flour
1 can consommé
½ cup Chablis wine

Cut the kidneys in walnut-size pieces. Remove the membranes. Sauté with the onion in butter or margarine. Remove the kidneys and set aside in a warm place.

Add the flour to the pan. Mix with the onions and add the consommé and wine. Simmer 10 minutes, stirring. Return the kidneys to the pan and heat. Serve in a ring of cooked rice, sprinkled with parsley.   *Serves 4.*

WELSH RABBIT

This may be the oldest of all cooked cheese dishes, and it makes a marvelous lunch. Substitute cream for the beer if you wish, but never call it a "Rarebit."

½ tablespoon Worcestershire sauce
⅛ teaspoon paprika
¼ teaspoon dry mustard
1 teaspoon salt
¾ cup beer, fresh or stale
1 pound sharp cheddar cheese
8 slices buttered toast

Mix the seasonings and add the beer. Put in a double boiler and heat until the beer is hot.

Grate the cheese and add to the beer. Stir (in one direction only), until cheese is melted and the mixture piping hot. Serve at once over freshly-made, buttered toast.   *Serves 4.*

SHERRIED CHICKEN BREASTS

We worked in a nice Florida restaurant one winter where this was the most popular item on the menu.

4 whole chicken breasts
¾ teaspoon salt
⅛ teaspoon pepper
2 tablespoons fresh lemon juice
3 tablespoons melted butter
½ cup dry sherry

Bone, skin and halve the chicken breasts. Place in a baking dish, but do not overlap. Sprinkle both sides with salt, pepper and lemon juice. Pour melted butter over each piece, rubbing it in with the back of a spoon. Pour sherry over the chicken.

Cover the baking dish with aluminum foil and place in a 400°F oven for 30 minutes. When done, the chicken will be white and spring back when pressed with finger. (Do not overcook, or the breasts will be dry and the flavor lost.)

Pour off the liquid from the baking pan and save. Keep the chicken warm while preparing the sauce (see below).

SAUCE

4 tablespoons butter
4 tablespoons flour
1½ cups light cream
liquid from baking pan (¾ cup)
1 teaspoon paprika
3 tablespoons grated Parmesan cheese

Cook the butter and flour together for 2 to 3 minutes. Stir in the chicken liquid from the baking pan and the cream. Cook over medium heat until smooth and thick, stirring constantly.

Spread the sauce over the chicken breasts; sprinkle with Parmesan cheese and paprika. Return to the oven and bake until the surface is golden brown — about 5 minutes.

Serves 4.

JELLIED CHICKEN LOAF

A nice, light, summer Sunday supper dish. (Don't try to say summer Sunday supper dish fast!)

> 2 2½-pound broilers or fryers
> 4 cups boiling water
> 1 onion, chopped
> 2 stalks celery, chopped
> 1 bay leaf
> 1 teaspoon salt
> 6 whole peppercorns

Cut the chicken into pieces. Wash and put in a large saucepan. Add the boiling water, chopped onion, celery, bay leaf, salt and pepper. Cover, bring to a boil and simmer for 1½ hours, or until the chicken is tender. Drain and reserve the liquid. Cool the chicken.

Remove the meat from the bones and cut into coarse pieces. Arrange in a 9x5x2¾-inch loaf pan.

Skim the fat from the liquid in which the chicken was cooked. Strain, and reduce to 2 cups by boiling, uncovered. Season to taste with salt and pepper and pour over chicken. Cool, then chill overnight to set.

Unmold and slice. Serve with Vinaigrette Sauce (page 66) or mayonnaise.   *Serves 6.*

CHICKEN PIE

Follow directions, make this right, and we'll guarantee you the finest chicken pie you ever tasted.

> 2 2- to 2½-pound broilers or fryers, cut up
> 2 carrots, sliced
> 1 large onion, chopped
> 3 or 4 stalks celery, including tops,
>   chopped
> 1 bay leaf
> ¼ teaspoon white pepper
> 2 tablespoons salt
> 3 quarts water

Bring the water to a boil. Add the vegetables, bay leaf, pepper and salt. When the water boils again, add the chicken, piece by piece. Lower the heat and simmer until the chicken is very tender — about 2½ hours. Cool quickly.

Remove the meat from the bones. Remove all skin and cut the meat into large bite-size pieces. Reserve. Return the bones and skin to the broth in which the chicken was cooked, simmering for ¾ hour. Strain the broth, adding salt and pepper to taste. Refrigerate the meat and the broth until ready to use.

Continue with . . .

> 4 tablespoons butter or margarine
> 4 tablespoons flour
> 2 cups chicken broth
> 1 cup light cream
> 1 egg
> 1 pound carrots, quartered and cooked
> 1 10-ounce package frozen peas, cooked
> 1 1-pound can tiny white onions,
>   drained
> 3 tablespoons fresh chopped parsley
> 12 wheat germ biscuits (see page 148)

Melt the butter or margarine in a good-sized saucepan. Stir in the flour. Skim the fat from the surface of the broth and add the broth alternately with the cream, stirring constantly. Bring to a boil. If the sauce is thicker than heavy cream, add a little more of each liquid.

Beat the egg thoroughly. Add a small quantity of the gravy to the egg, then pour back into kettle. Add the chicken, carrots, peas, onions, and chopped parsley. Taste; add salt and pepper if needed.

Pour the mixture into a 2-quart casserole and place in a 425°F oven. Heat until it bubbles vigorously. As quickly as possible, arrange unbaked biscuits on top of the pie and return to the oven for 10 to 15 minutes or until the biscuits are done. *Serves 8.*

PAELLA VALENCIANA

Food for the gods. This isn't hard to make; it just takes time. And it deserves to be done in a paella pan.

2 2-pound broiler-fryers, cut up, with
   giblets
2 teaspoons salt, divided
1 carrot, cut in small pieces
1 onion, chopped
1 bay leaf
1 tablespoon chopped parsley
8 whole black peppercorns
3 cups water
½ cup olive oil
3 cloves garlic, minced
1 large green pepper, cut in julienne
   strips
1 teaspoon crumbled saffron
½ teaspoon pepper
1½ dozen whole clams
1½ cups raw, long-grain white rice
3 cups fresh tomatoes, peeled and
   coarsely chopped
1 pound shrimp, cooked, shelled and
   deveined
2 tablespoons finely chopped parsley

In a large saucepan, combine the chicken giblets, ½ teaspoon salt, carrot, onion, bay leaf, parsley, black peppercorns and water. Bring to a boil. Reduce the heat and simmer, covered, for 40 minutes.

While this is cooking, slowly heat the olive oil in a large dutch oven or paella pan. Slowly brown the chicken in the hot oil, a few pieces at a time. Remove from the oil.

Now sauté in the hot oil the garlic, green pepper, saffron and ½ teaspoon pepper for about 5 minutes. Arrange the browned chicken pieces on top.

Drain and discard the giblets and vegetables, reserving the liquid. You should have 3 cups. (If not, add clam juice or cooking liquid from the shrimp to make up the difference.) Bring to a boil over medium heat. Stir in the rice and the remaining 1½ teaspoons of salt with a fork, mixing well. Bring back to the boil. Add to the chicken pieces and bake, covered, for 1 hour at 350°F. Stir the rice every 15 or 20 minutes.

Scrub clams thoroughly and add to the casserole with tomatoes and shrimp. Bake 15 minutes longer, or until the clams open. Sprinkle with parsley.   *Serves 6-8.*

CORNISH HENS WITH PECAN STUFFING AND PORT WINE SAUCE

This elegant combination of good looks and good taste is a real showpiece.

> 4 Cornish hens
> 2 tablespoons butter or margarine, melted

Brush the hens with butter or margarine and dredge with flour. Stuff the cavities with Pecan Stuffing (see below) but do not pack. Place uncovered in a 450°F oven for 45 minutes or until tender. Transfer to a heated serving platter. Serve with Port Wine Sauce (see below).

Serves 4.

PECAN STUFFING

> 4 tablespoons butter or margarine
> ¼ cup onion, chopped
> ½ teaspoon salt
> 1½ cups cooked white rice
> ½ cup pecan halves

Sauté the onion in butter or margarine. Add the other ingredients. Toss lightly.

PORT WINE SAUCE

> ¼ cup butter or margarine
> ¼ cup minced onion
> 3 tablespoons flour
> 1 tablespoon meat-extract paste or 3 bouillon cubes
> 3 tablespoons currant jelly
> 1 cup dark sweet cherries, drained and pitted
> ¾ cup port wine
> 1 cup water

Cook the onion in butter, stirring, until tender; remove from the heat. Stir in the flour, meat-extract paste, currant jelly and water. Cook, stirring, over medium heat until thickened. Add the wine and cherries and heat just to boiling, stirring gently so as not to hurt the cherries.

ROAST DUCKLING ORIENTAL

Another gourmet delight, where the secret is in the sauce. Note it calls for fresh *orange juice and* fresh *orange sections.*

>1 duckling, 4 to 5 pounds, quartered
>giblets and neck
>2 cups water
>¼ cup soy sauce
>1 tablespoon sugar
>½ teaspoon salt
>1 teaspoon ground ginger
>¼ teaspoon paprika
>1 clove garlic, minced
>2 cups broth
>1 cup fresh orange juice
>2 tablespoons cornstarch
>¼ cup water
>2 cups fresh orange sections

Wash and dry the duckling; remove any pinfeathers. In a shallow, open roasting pan, roast the duckling skin side up for 1¼ hours at 350°F.

Make duckling broth by simmering the giblets and neck (not the liver) in 2 cups water, covered, for 1½ hours. Strain.

When the duckling is done, transfer it from the roasting pan to a heated serving platter. Pour off the drippings from the pan. Put the strained broth and orange juice in the pan and bring to boil. Mix the soy sauce, salt, ginger, sugar, paprika, garlic and cornstarch in the ¼ cup water. Add to the liquids in pan and simmer, stirring, for 10 minutes.

Section fresh oranges. Remove the membranes and seeds. Add the sections to the sauce and simmer another 5 minutes. Pour over the duckling.   *Serves 4.*

OVEN FRIED FISH FILLETS

An excellent way to cook fish — better than ordinary fry-
ing. Doesn't smell up the kitchen either.

> 2 pounds fish fillets
> 1 tablespoon salt
> 1 cup milk
> 1 cup crushed cornflakes
> ¼ cup butter or margarine, melted
> lemon wedges

Cut the fillets into serving pieces. Add the salt to the milk. Dip the fillets in milk and roll in the cornflake crumbs. Place on a shallow, well-greased baking pan, skin down. Sprinkle each piece with melted butter or margarine.

Bake in a 500°F oven for 10-12 minutes, or until the fish flakes. Garnish with lemon wedges.   *Serves 4.*

HEARTY FISHERMAN'S STEW

Make this with frozen fish if you can't get fresh; it will taste
almost as good.

> 2 pounds haddock or codfish fillets
> 1½ cups chopped celery
> ½ cup chopped onion
> 1 clove garlic, minced
> ¼ cup butter or margarine
> 1 12-ounce can peeled tomatoes,
>   undrained
> 1 8-ounce can tomato sauce
> 2 teaspoons salt
> ½ teaspoon paprika
> ½ teaspoon chili powder
> ¼ teaspoon pepper
> 1 8-ounce package spaghetti

2 cups boiling water
¼ cup Parmesan cheese, grated or shredded

Cut the fish into 1-inch pieces. Sauté the celery, onion and garlic in butter or margarine in a large deep pan until tender. Add the tomatoes, tomato sauce and seasonings. Bring to a simmer. Cover. Cook slowly for 20 minutes. Add the uncooked spaghetti and boiling water. Stir, cover and cook slowly about 10 minutes or until the spaghetti is almost tender. Add the fish. Cover. Cook slowly until fish flakes easily with a fork (about 10 minutes). Serve hot, sprinkled with Parmesan cheese.

Serves 6.

JIFFY BROILED HADDOCK

Fish — especially frozen — is often on the bland side. Made this way it has a little more character.

2 pounds haddock fillets, fresh or frozen
2 tablespoons vegetable oil
2 tablespoons soy sauce
2 tablespoons Worcestershire sauce
1 teaspoon paprika
½ teaspoon chili powder
½ teaspoon garlic powder
4 or 5 drops Tabasco sauce
lemon wedges for garnish

Thaw the fillets if frozen. Place them in a single layer, skin side down, on a well-greased broil-and-serve platter, 10x16 inches. Combine the remaining ingredients and pour over the fillets.

Broil about 4 inches from the heat source for 10 to 15 minutes, or until the fillets flake easily when tested with a fork. Baste once during broiling with the sauce in the pan. Serve garnished with lemon wedges.

Serves 6.

FIFTH OF JULY SALMON LOAF

Poached salmon is a tradition on the Fourth of July in New England. So it follows that this Salmon Loaf is served on the Fifth. Enjoy it any time, no matter where you live.

> 2 envelopes unflavored gelatin
> 2 pounds cooked fresh salmon, skinned
>   and boned
> 3 cups finely diced celery
> ½ cup minced green pepper
> 4 pimientos, chopped
> juice of 2 lemons
> 1½ cups mayonnaise
> 1½ teaspoons salt
> ¼ teaspoon pepper

Sprinkle the gelatin on ½ cup cold water in the top of a double boiler. Let stand 5 minutes, then dissolve over hot water, stirring. Add the salmon, lightly crumbled. Mix in the remaining ingredients. Pack into an oiled loaf pan and chill overnight. Unmold on greens. Serve with Green Mayonnaise (see below).   *Serves 6-8.*

GREEN MAYONNAISE

> 8 sprigs parsley
> 8 leaves spinach
> 8 sprigs watercress
> 1 cup mayonnaise
> ⅛ teaspoon nutmeg

Cover the parsley, spinach and watercress with boiling water. Let stand 5 minutes. Drain. Place in ice water and drain again. Rub through a fine sieve and add to the mayonnaise. Add nutmeg.   *Serves 6-8.*

ROMAN SCAMPI

Ready for a real challenge? This one isn't cheap, and it isn't easy, but pull it off and your reputation is assured. The tricky part is broiling the shrimp; watch carefully or you'll burn them.

1½ pounds raw jumbo shrimp
1 cup Chablis wine
1 clove garlic, minced
1 bay leaf
2 teaspoons grated lemon peel
⅛ teaspoon Tabasco sauce
4 tablespoons unsalted butter
paprika

Shell the shrimp, leaving on the tails. Devein; split down the back. Marinate for 24 hours in a marinade of the wine, garlic, bay leaf, lemon peel, and Tabasco. Turn frequently.

Remove from the marinade, arrange on a broiling pan, dot with butter and sprinkle with paprika. Broil for 10 minutes, basting with juice from the marinade. Be careful not to scorch.

Serve with the marinade which has been strained and heated.

Serves 4.

SHRIMP AND CRABMEAT CASSEROLE

We can't explain why, exactly, but this is the *most popular dish we've ever served.* Nobody *has ever failed to ask for the recipe. It's also easy to make and can be put together in advance, then baked at the last minute.*

½ pound macaroni
1 tablespoon salt
1 tablespoon vegetable oil
4 tablespoons butter or margarine
½ pound fresh mushrooms, sliced
2 tablespoons butter or margarine
1 cup light cream
1 10-ounce can cream of mushroom
    soup
¾ cup grated sharp cheddar cheese
1 pound cooked shrimp, shelled and
    deveined
1 cup cooked crabmeat

1 cup soft bread crumbs
1 tablespoon butter or margarine

Add the salt and vegetable oil to 3 quarts boiling water. Add the macaroni and boil rapidly for 10 minutes. Drain and toss with 4 tablespoons butter or margarine.

Sauté the mushrooms in 2 tablespoons butter or margarine for about 5 minutes, shaking the pan frequently. Mix the cream, mushroom soup and cheddar cheese together and add to the macaroni. Add the mushrooms, shrimp and crabmeat, which has been cut into bite-size pieces.

Place in a buttered casserole, top with soft bread crumbs which have been tossed with the 1 tablespoon melted butter or margarine. Bake in a 350°F oven for 25 minutes. *Serves 6.*

BAKED JUMBO SHRIMP

Every bit as good as Roman Scampi but easier to make. (You don't need to watch it so carefully.)

2¼ pounds large raw shrimp
½ cup butter or margarine
1 teaspoon salt
6 cloves garlic, minced
⅓ cup chopped parsley
3 teaspoons grated lemon peel
3 tablespoons lemon juice
lemon wedges

Shell the shrimp, devein, wash, and drain on a paper towel. Melt the butter or margarine in a 13x9x2-inch baking dish. Add the salt, garlic and half of the parsley. Arrange the shrimp in a single layer in a baking dish. Bake uncovered in a 400°F oven for 5 minutes.

Turn the shrimp and sprinkle with the lemon peel, lemon juice and remaining parsley. Bake 8-10 minutes more, or just until tender. Arrange on a heated platter. Pour the garlic butter over all. Garnish with lemon wedges. *Serves 6.*

CRABMEAT CREPES

There are few dishes more elegant!

    1 pound cooked, flaked crabmeat
    3 cans condensed cream of shrimp soup
    4 tablespoons butter or margarine
    ½ pound fresh mushrooms, sliced
    4 tablespoons dry sherry
    4 tablespoons brandy
    ½ teaspoon salt
    ⅛ teaspoon nutmeg
    1 tablespoon lemon juice
    4 tablespoons light cream
   24 Crêpes (see below)

Combine the crabmeat and soup. Cook the mushrooms in butter or margarine over medium heat until tender. Add to the soup mixture. Add all the remaining ingredients except the light cream.

Using half of the mixture, fill 24 crêpes (see below), roll, and place in a baking dish. Stir the cream into the second half of the mixture and pour around the crêpes. Bake in a 300°F oven for 35 minutes.   *Serves 8.*

CREPES

    1½ cups all-purpose flour
    ¾ teaspoon salt
    2 teaspoons baking powder
    3 eggs
    1⅓ cups milk
    ⅔ cup water
    3 tablespoons butter or margarine

Sift the flour with the salt and baking powder. Beat the

eggs, and add to the milk and water. Make a well in the dry ingredients and pour in the liquid. Combine quickly. Do not overmix.

Heat 1 tablespoon butter or margarine in a 5-inch skillet. Add the remaining butter or margarine as needed while cooking the crêpes. Pour in a small quantity of batter, enough to spread thinly over the bottom of the skillet. Cook over moderate heat until the pancake is brown underneath, then turn and brown the other side lightly. The crêpes may be stacked with foil between each one until ready to be stuffed.   *Makes 24 crêpes.*

DINNER PARTY SCALLOPS

A favorite with fish lovers. Quick and easy to prepare, but looks as though you went to a lot of trouble. Take the credit, anyway.

> 2 pounds scallops (bay or sea)
> 1 large clove garlic, minced
> ¾ cup butter or margarine
> 2 tablespoons minced onions
> 3 tablespoons fresh chopped parsley
> ½ teaspoon salt
> ¼ teaspoon pepper

Wash and drain the scallops. Wipe dry. Place in a single layer in an ovenproof dish.

Melt the butter or margarine; add the garlic, onions, parsley, salt and pepper. Mix well and pour over the scallops. Let stand for 2 or 3 hours.

Broil under a moderate flame about 3½ minutes on each side, or until the scallops look nice and brown.

Serves 4.

LOBSTER TAIL CASSEROLE

Another great buffet dish. Easy to make and you can do most of the work well ahead of time.

> 10 frozen lobster tails (8 ounces)
> ¼ cup butter or margarine
> ¼ cup flour
> 2 teaspoons salt
> ½ teaspoon pepper
> 2 teaspoons paprika
> 1 tablespoon onion, minced
> 1 teaspoon Angostura bitters
> 2½ cups milk
> 2½ cups light cream
> ⅓ cup dry sherry
> 12 ounces medium egg noodles

Cover the frozen lobster tails with boiling salted water. Bring to a boil and simmer 5 minutes.

Drop the noodles into 3 quarts of boiling water to which you have added 1 tablespoon salt and 1 tablespoon salad oil. Boil for 5 minutes and drain.

Melt the butter or margarine; stir in the flour, salt, paprika, pepper, onion and bitters. Add the milk and cream, and stir the sauce until thickened. Add the sherry and the lobster tails, cut into bite-size pieces. Put into a 3-quart buttered casserole and mix with the cooked noodles. Top with buttered bread crumbs. Bake at 375°F for 35 minutes. *Serves 8-10.*

DEVILED CLAMS

A great luncheon dish. Serve with a green salad and hot biscuits.

4 tablespoons butter or margarine
1 teaspoon minced onion
1 chopped green pepper
½ pound fresh mushrooms, sliced
4 tablespoons flour
2 cups milk
½ teaspoon salt
¼ teaspoon celery seed
4 7-ounce cans minced clams, drained
¾ cup dry bread crumbs
2 tablespoons butter or margarine

Melt the butter or margarine and sauté the onion, pepper and mushrooms until limp. Sprinkle with flour and mix well. Gradually add the milk and cook, stirring, until thickened and bubbly. Add the salt and celery seed. Add the drained clams and divide the mixture into individual baking dishes, well greased. Sprinkle with dry bread crumbs and dot with butter or margarine. Bake at 350°F for 30 minutes.

Makes 12 appetizer servings or 6 luncheon-size portions.

VEGETABLES

When your mother insisted you eat your vegetables, she knew what she was doing. Fresh vegetables are chock full of vitamins, minerals, and other good things essential to your health and well-being. Yet their nutritive value — and flavor — are very easily destroyed. The faster a vegetable gets from the garden to the table the better. And the more gentle the cooking process the better.

Few restaurants serve vegetables that are fit to eat. Not because they don't know how; the logistics of the restaurant business are such that it's difficult to do the job right. That's why many restaurants, even some very good ones, don't even try. They just serve potatoes and a salad, both of which are easier to prepare and "hold."

Follow these tips and your vegetables will look better, taste better and be better for you.

1. Don't let them soak in water before cooking. The

water will absorb nutrients and flavor. Over-exposure to air will do the same.

2. Prepare them just before cooking and no longer in advance than necessary.

3. Cook them in their skins if possible and cook them whole if possible.

4. Don't overcook. Mushy vegetables are out. Try cooking only until tender, even a little crisp.

5. Get your vegetables as fresh as possible. Freshness here is more important than with any other food. We age our meat on purpose. Many fruits have protective skins that keep goodness locked in for long periods of time. But most vegetables start to deteriorate the minute they leave the garden. If you can't get them fresh, get them frozen.

Can you scratch out a few square feet of land around your house? Start a vegetable garden, even a small one. The rewards are great.

There are many different ways to cook vegetables. But here is —

THE VERY BEST WAY TO COOK VEGETABLES

Steam them! All you need is an inexpensive little gadget called, appropriately enough, a vegetable steamer, which is quite big enough for the average small family. After you prepare the vegetables, you put them in the steamer and put the steamer in a pot with a little water. The water never touches the vegetables because the steamer stands on little legs. The vegetables are cooked by steam, or more correctly, by hot water vapors.

You don't really know what your favorite vegetable tastes like until you've tried cooking it this way. Virtually none of the flavor or nutrition is lost. And the color is beautiful. Mix or match in the same pot. No problem.

Nothing is perfect, and the vegetable steamer is no exception. But its faults are few and easily overcome. First, they're not too big, so you may need two or three if yours is a larger family. Second, you don't use much water, so it's likely to boil away if you don't watch it.

A pressure cooker or "waterless" cooker does almost as well as a steamer. If you use either of these two, save what little water residue there is left and add to soup.

THE VERY *WORST* WAY TO COOK VEGETABLES

Peel, cut in small pieces, leave exposed on the kitchen counter for an hour or two. Then put in a pot filled with water, add plenty of salt and some baking soda. (Try to do this early in the day, maybe even in the morning.)

Some time in the afternoon, bring to a boil and continue boiling until the vegetables are soft and mushy. Leave the vegetables in the pot and put the pot on back of the stove until meal time. Then remove the vegetables from the water and serve.

What has this process accomplished?

Exposure to air and water has destroyed most of the flavor and food value. The baking soda preserved some of the color but effectively killed what little food value remained. Lots of salt made sure there was no natural flavor left.

HOW TO COOK VEGETABLES IN ADVANCE
SO YOU CAN SERVE THEM LATER
(and still have something worth eating)

STEAM your vegetables until they are about 75% done. Then immerse in cold water to stop the cooking process. Drain well and refrigerate.

When ready to serve, you have two ways to go. You can plunge the vegetables in boiling water for a couple of minutes, or you can sauté them in butter or oil. We prefer the latter method. Tastier.

Either way, the vegetables retain their color, flavor and nutrition. Restaurants that serve good vegetables generally follow either of these methods.

ASPARAGUS POLONAISE

Just everybody *does Asparagus Hollandaise. Asparagus Polonaise is a lot easier and very pleasant for a change. You serve it with an airy remark such as: "I thought you'd enjoy the asparagus Polonaise. Hollandaise gets to be* such *a bore, don't you think?"*

> 2 pounds fresh asparagus
> 4 tablespoons butter
> 2 cups coarse soft bread crumbs
> 2 tablespoons chopped parsley

Remove the tough stalk ends of the asparagus. Clean off the scales and any sand under them. Wash. Arrange the stalks in a shallow pan and cover with water and 1 teaspoon salt. Bring to a boil and cook for 6 to 8 minutes or until tender crisp. Lift out carefully with slotted spoon or tongs. Arrange in a heated shallow serving dish.

Melt the butter in a small frying pan and stir in the bread crumbs, tossing until the crumbs are golden. Stir in the chopped parsley. Sprinkle the mixture over the asparagus and serve at once. *Serves 6.*

BAKED BEANS WITH RUM

A lot of people prefer these to Boston Baked because they're not as sweet. Or maybe it's the rum?

2 pounds dried pea beans
1 onion stuck with 3 cloves
1 tablespoon salt
¾ pound lean salt pork
¾ pound smoked ham
3 onions, chopped
3 cloves garlic, minced
2 teaspoons dry mustard
¼ cup dark rum

Cover the beans with water and soak overnight. Drain and add fresh water to 3 inches above the beans. Add the onion with cloves and the salt. Boil 5 minutes. Skim, reduce the heat and simmer for 30 minutes, or until tender (not mushy).

Put the salt pork in water and bring to a boil. Lower the heat and simmer for 30 minutes. Remove the pork and cut in small pieces. Cut the smoked ham in julienne strips.

Blend the mustard with a little of the bean liquid. Place a layer of beans in the bottom of a large baking dish. Add a layer of pork, ham, onion and garlic. Repeat the layers, ending with beans on top. Add the mustard mixture and enough bean liquid to come to the top of the baking dish. Bake at 300°F for about 4 hours. Add more liquid if necessary.

Remove from the oven and pour the rum over the beans. Return to the oven and bake for another 45 minutes, or until brown and bubbly.   *Serves 10-12.*

CARROT SOUFFLE

Carrots are usually dull. Here, they take on a sparkling new personality.

    4 medium carrots
    ½ teaspoon salt
    3 tablespoons butter or margarine
    3 tablespoons flour
    1 cup milk
    ½ teaspoon salt
    ⅛ teaspoon pepper
    4 eggs, separated

Scrape and slice the carrots. Cook in boiling water to cover, with ½ teaspoon salt, until tender. Drain and mash. Force through a fine sieve or whirl in the blender. Measure; you should have 1 cup.

Melt the butter or margarine in a skillet. Blend in the flour. Gradually add the milk and cook, stirring, until smooth and thickened. Add the second ½ teaspoon salt and the ⅛ teaspoon pepper and cool slightly.

Beat the egg whites until stiff but not dry. Set aside.

Beat the egg yolks until light and lemon-colored. Add to the cooled mixture. Add the carrot pulp and blend. Fold half the egg whites into the carrot mixture. Gently fold in the remaining whites.

Butter a 2-quart soufflé dish and fill with the mixture. Bake at 375°F for 30 minutes or until puffed and lightly browned.

Serves 4.

CARROT BAKE

For the many people who are shy about serving carrots to company.

> 9 or 10 large carrots
> ¼ cup chopped green pepper
> ¼ cup chopped onion
> 4 tablespoons butter or margarine
> 2 tablespoons flour
> 1 cup milk
> 2 tablespoons sugar
> ½ teaspoon salt
> 1 tablespoon butter or margarine
> ½ cup soft bread crumbs

Peel, slice and steam the carrots until tender. Mash. Sauté the green pepper and onion in the 4 tablespoons butter or margarine. Stir in the flour, milk, salt and sugar. Cook until thickened. Add the mashed carrots and put in a greased casserole.

Melt the 1 tablespoon butter or margarine and in this toss the crumbs until golden. Spread over the carrots. Bake at 350°F for 30 minutes.   *Serves 6.*

CELERY SOUFFLE

Who said celery should always be relegated to the Salad Department?

> 4 slices soft bread
> ½ cup milk
> 4 tablespoons butter or margarine
> ½ cup finely chopped celery
> 2 teaspoons minced onion
> 4 eggs, separated
> ½ teaspoon salt
> ⅛ teaspoon pepper

Cut the bread into small cubes and soften in the milk.

Melt the butter or margarine in a skillet. Add the celery and onion and cook for 3 minutes. Add the bread and milk and heat thoroughly, then beat until smooth. Remove from the heat.

Beat the egg yolks and add to the skillet, beating well. Add the seasonings. Beat the egg whites until stiff and fold into the mixture.

Pour into a well-buttered 1-quart casserole, set in a pan of hot water, and bake at 375°F for 30 minutes. *Serves 4.*

CHEESE SPINACH PIE

It sounds terrible; it tastes great. When you announce what it is, better make up your own description.

    1 pound fresh spinach, cooked and
      chopped
    1 cup cottage cheese
    2 eggs, beaten
    1 teaspoon caraway seed
    1 teaspoon salt
    ⅛ teaspoon pepper
    ⅛ teaspoon nutmeg

Mix all the ingredients together. Put in a small shallow casserole or 8-inch pie pan and sprinkle with Topping (see below).

TOPPING

    1 slice bread, crumbled
    2 tablespoons butter or margarine
    2 tablespoons grated Parmesan cheese
    2 teaspoons chopped parsley
    ⅛ teaspoon paprika

Toss the crumbs in butter or margarine until golden. Add the cheese, parsley and paprika. Spread over the spinach mixture. Bake in a 350°F oven for 20 minutes.

Serves 4.

FLUFFY CORN CAKES

Generally speaking, canned corn is a drag. But good fresh corn is available for such a short time each year. What's a corn lover to do? Here's one good answer.

> 4 eggs, separated
> 2 cups cream-style canned corn
> ¾ teaspoon salt
> 2 tablespoons butter or margarine, melted
> 1 cup cracker crumbs
> 1 teaspoon baking powder
> 3 tablespoons vegetable oil

Beat the egg whites until stiff. Beat the yolks slightly and add the corn, salt and butter or margarine. Mix the cracker crumbs and baking powder and combine with the corn mixture. Fold in the egg whites.

Fry by spoonfuls in hot oil until golden brown on each side. *Serves 6.*

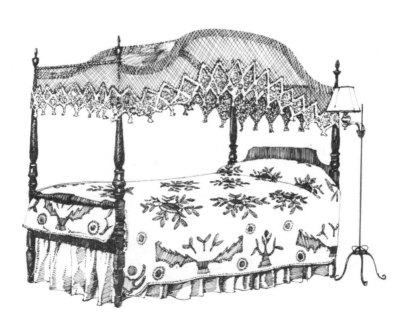

MARINATED EGGPLANT

A good side dish. We've tried it with almost everything, but it seems to go with lamb best of all.

> 2 large eggplants
> 1½ teaspoons salt
> ¼ cup white vinegar or dry white wine
> ¼ cup olive oil
> 4 garlic cloves, diced

Peel the eggplants and cut into 2-inch cubes. Cover with water and boil for 8 to 10 minutes or until soft (but not mushy). Drain.

In a large bowl with a tight-fitting lid, mix the salt, vinegar or wine, oil and diced garlic. Add the eggplant and store in the refrigerator for at least 2 days. *Serves 8.*

CREAMY MUSHROOM CASSEROLE

A great accompaniment for chicken or turkey.

> ⅓ cup soft butter or margarine
> 1 tablespoon chopped fresh parsley
> 1 tablespoon grated onion
> 1 tablespoon prepared mustard
> 1 teaspoon salt
> ⅛ teaspoon cayenne pepper
> ⅛ teaspoon nutmeg
> 1½ teaspoons flour
> 1 pound washed fresh mushrooms
> 1 cup heavy cream

Slice the mushrooms, stems on, and place a layer on bottom of a 1½-quart greased casserole. Mix together the butter or margarine, parsley, onion, mustard, salt, pepper, nutmeg and flour. Dot the first layer of sliced mushrooms with half this mixture. Add a second layer of mushrooms and top with the rest of the butter mixture.

Pour the cream over all, then bake uncovered at 350°F for 1 hour. *Serves 4.*

MUSHROOMS AU GRATIN

You think it's impossible to improve on sautéed mushrooms?

>1 pound fresh mushrooms
>4 tablespoons butter or margarine
>1½ tablespoons flour
>¾ cup chicken broth
>¼ teaspoon dry oregano
>1 tablespoon chopped parsley
>1 teaspoon salt
>⅛ teaspoon ground black pepper
>¼ cup heavy cream
>1 tablespoon dry sherry
>2 tablespoons grated Parmesan cheese
>¼ cup fresh bread crumbs

Wash the mushrooms and remove stems. Chop the stems fine and slice the caps. Melt butter or margarine in a large skillet and cook the mushrooms for 15 minutes, stirring occasionally.

Stir in the flour and blend well. Gradually stir in the chicken broth. When the sauce is smooth, add the oregano, parsley, salt and pepper. Cook, stirring, for 5 minutes. Stir in the cream and sherry and cook 3 minutes longer.

Put the mushrooms and sauce into a small casserole, sprinkle with cheese mixed with bread crumbs, and bake for 20 minutes at 350°F. *Serves 4.*

HOLIDAY CREAMED ONIONS

It's the raisins and the sherry that do it for this dish.

1½ pounds small boiling onions
1 quart water
1 teaspoon salt
6 tablespoons butter or margarine
6 tablespoons flour
1¼ cups water from boiled onions
2¼ cups light cream
¼ cup white seedless raisins
¼ cup dry sherry
dash paprika

Cover the unpeeled onions with hot water. Bring to a boil and remove from the heat. When the onions are cool enough to handle, peel, scraping the root ends (do not cut). The skins will slip off easily.

Bring the 1 quart water and salt to a boil and add the peeled onions. Cook until barely tender, about 15 minutes. Drain, reserving the 1¼ cups onion water.

Heat the butter or margarine, mix in the flour and stir until bubbly. Add the 1¼ cups onion water and cream. Bring to a boil and simmer for 10 minutes, stirring.

Heat the sherry and add the raisins. Let stand for 5 minutes. Add this to the sauce with the drained onions. Heat but do not boil. Serve with a dusting of paprika.

Serves 6-8.

CREAMED ONION PIE

An unusual vegetable dish. Try it on your next buffet.

CRUST

> 2 cups flour
> ½ cup shortening
> ½ teaspoon salt
> 5 tablespoons water
> ½ cup sharp cheddar cheese, grated

Cut the shortening into the flour and salt until the mixture is the consistency of coarse meal. Add the grated cheese. Add the water and mix with a fork until you can make the dough into a ball. Chill.

FILLING

> 4 medium-size onions
> 1 teaspoon salt
> ½ cup evaporated milk
> 1½ teaspoons butter or margarine
> 1½ teaspoons flour

Slice the onions (not too thin). Cover with cold water and add the salt. Bring to a quick boil. Drain, saving ½ cup of the cooking water. Add the evaporated milk.

Melt the butter or margarine and blend in the flour. Add the cooking water and milk, stirring until thickened and smooth. Add the onions, mixing lightly.

Divide the pastry into two parts and roll out one to fit a 9-inch pie plate. Add the creamed onions. Roll out the second half of the pastry and cover the pie. Make slits in the top crust and seal the edges well. Bake 40 minutes at 350°F. *Serves 6 as a side dish.*

BAKED PARSNIPS

Served this way, they generally evoke a smile rather than a frown.

>   1 pound parsnips, peeled
>   ½ teaspoon salt
>   2 apples, peeled, cored and chopped
>   1 cup apple juice
>   3 tablespoons brown sugar
>   ⅛ teaspoon nutmeg

Trim the tops off the parsnips. Cut in half lengthwise and remove any woody core. Place in a skillet and cover with water. Add the salt. Bring to a boil and cook until barely tender, about 10 minutes.

Drain well and place in a baking dish. Sprinkle with chopped apple, then pour over the apple juice mixed with the brown sugar and nutmeg.

Bake at 350°F for 20 minutes, or until the apples are done.   *Serves 4-6.*

SPINACH DELICIOUS

Means just what it says: delicious. And that's the truth.

>   1 pound fresh spinach, cooked
>   2 tablespoons butter or margarine
>   ¼ cup light cream
>   2 tablespoons horseradish
>   ½ teaspoon salt
>   ⅛ teaspoon pepper
>   1 hard-cooked egg, sieved

Chop the spinach. Add all remaining ingredients except the egg and heat. Garnish with sieved hard-cooked egg.   *Serves 4-5.*

SPINACH SOUFFLE

The only way we know to turn a spinach hater into a spinach lover.

> 3 tablespoons butter
> 3 tablespoons flour
> 1¼ cups milk
> ½ teaspoon salt
> dash Tabasco sauce
> 5 eggs, separated
> 3 tablespoons cheddar cheese, grated
> 1¼ cups cooked chopped spinach, well
>   drained

Melt the butter and blend in the flour and seasonings. When the mixture is smooth, stir in the milk, mixing well. Cook over low heat, stirring, until thick and smooth. Gradually beat in the well-beaten egg yolks, a little at a time. Add the spinach. Cool.

Beat the egg whites until stiff but not dry. Fold into the spinach mixture. Pour into a greased 2-quart soufflé dish. Sprinkle the top with the grated cheese and bake at 350°F for 40 minutes, or until the top is brown and the soufflé nicely puffed. *Serves 4.*

GLAZED ACORN SQUASH

Tasty, nutritious, economical and easy to prepare. What more could one ask?

> 3 acorn squash
> 6 tablespoons maple syrup
> 6 tablespoons light cream
> 6 teaspoons butter or margarine

Wash the squash and cut them in half. Remove the seeds and the stringy part. Place, cut side up, in a large shallow baking dish containing ½ inch of hot water.

Heat the cream to the boiling point. Add the maple syrup. Pour evenly into each of the six acorn squash hollows. Dot each squash half with 1 teaspoon butter or margarine. Cover.

Bake at 400°F for 30 minutes. Uncover and bake 15 minutes longer, or until lightly brown.   *Serves 6.*

PENNSYLVANIA DUTCH TOMATOES

Dare to be different — try these for breakfast with crisp bacon.

    4 tablespoons butter or margarine
    6 firm tomatoes, red or green
    4 tablespoons flour
    1 teaspoon salt
    ⅛ teaspoon pepper
    3 tablespoons brown sugar
    1 cup heavy cream

Cut the tomatoes into thick slices; dip in flour mixed with salt and pepper. Sprinkle with brown sugar.

Heat the butter or margarine in a large skillet. Add the tomatoes and cook slowly. Turn once and sprinkle again with brown sugar. When the tomatoes are tender, add cream and cook until it bubbles. Arrange the tomatoes on a serving platter and pour the sauce over them.

Serves 6.

TURNIP SOUFFLE

Dress a turnip up like this and you can take it anywhere.

1 pound white turnips
3 tablespoons butter or margarine
3 tablespoons flour
½ teaspoon salt
⅛ teaspoon pepper
1 tablespoon grated onion
½ cup heavy cream
4 eggs, separated

Peel the turnips and cut in ¼-inch slices. Cook in boiling water to cover for 15 minutes, or until soft. Drain, reserving ½ cup of liquid. Force the turnips through a fine sieve or food mill, or purée in the blender.

Melt the butter or margarine and blend in the flour, seasonings and onion. Gradually add the cream and turnip liquid. Add the turnip purée and cook, stirring until thickened. Add the egg yolks, beaten until thick and lemon-colored. Then fold in stiffly beaten egg whites.

Pour into a well-greased 2-quart casserole and bake, covered, at 350°F for 15 minutes. Remove the cover and bake an additional 20-25 minutes or until delicately browned.   *Serves 5-6.*

SCALLOPED CUCUMBERS AND ZUCCHINI

This goes very well with almost any dinner you put on the table.

1 large cucumber
4 small zucchini
5 slices bread, crumbled
3 tablespoons butter or margarine

1 teaspoon salt
⅛ teaspoon pepper
1 cup milk

Peel and slice the cucumber. Scrub and slice the zucchini, but do not peel.

On the bottom of a 6-cup casserole, spread 3 slices of the crumbled bread. Arrange a layer of cucumber and zucchini over the bread. Dot this with 1 tablespoon butter or margarine; sprinkle with salt and pepper. Follow with another layer of vegetables, dot with 1 tablespoon butter and sprinkle with seasonings. Cover with crumbs from the remaining 2 slices of bread, and dot with the remaining tablespoon of butter or margarine. Pour the milk over all.

Bake for 45 minutes in a 350°F oven. *Serves 6.*

POTATOES, GRAINS
AND CEREALS

When most people feel the need to lose a few pounds, the first thing they do is lay off the desserts — and the starches.

Well, it's O.K. to give up the sweets. Most of us get all the natural sugar we need if we eat right. And we can all get along very well without the starches found in bleached white flour and polished white rice.

But don't leave potatoes and the natural grains and cereals off your diet. They're good guys; they're rich in protein, vitamins and minerals. You *need* them. Besides, they taste good. And they really don't contain that many calories.

Remember, an average-size potato has only about 100 calories — if you leave off the butter, sour cream and fancy dressings.

FRIED BARLEY

When you can't get wild rice — or don't want to pay the price — this is a very acceptable substitute.

⅓ cup butter or margarine
¼ cup chopped onion
3½ cups cooked quick barley
½ teaspoon salt
¼ teaspoon pepper

Melt the butter in a frying pan and sauté the onion until lightly browned, about 5 minutes, stirring occasionally. Add the cooked barley (cook according to package directions), salt and pepper. Fry until the butter is absorbed, about 8 minutes, stirring occasionally.

Serves 6.

HONEY ORANGE MUESLI

Our version of a natural breakfast food called Bircher-muesli which was developed by a Swiss nutritionist.

2 cups quick or old-fashioned oats, uncooked
1 cup milk
1 teaspoon salt
½ cup orange juice
¼ cup honey
½ cup raisins
½ cup chopped dates
1 cup chopped apples
1 cup chopped walnuts or pecans

Combine the oats, milk and salt in a bowl; cover and refrigerate overnight. Just before serving, add the remaining ingredients. If desired, drizzle a little more honey on the top and more milk or cream.   *6 servings.*

GOLDEN POTATO BAKE

Goes very well with ham.

2 pounds potatoes
1 orange, rind and juice
6 eggs
4 tablespoons butter
1 cup light cream
2 tablespoons sugar
½ teaspoon salt
2 teaspoons baking powder

Peel the potatoes and cook until tender in boiling, salted water. Put through a ricer or mash. Cool.

Beat the eggs and add to them the orange juice and rind. Melt the butter, and blend with the cream and sugar; then add salt and baking powder. Fold everything together with the cooled potatoes and mix thoroughly. Put in a buttered oven dish. Bake for 1 hour in a 350°F oven. *Serves 8.*

MASHED POTATO CASSEROLE

A very tasty dish that you can do ahead of time and pop into the oven at the last minute. Good for a buffet.

10 medium-size potatoes, peeled
1 cup sour cream
1 cup cottage cheese
1 tablespoon grated onion
½ cup butter or margarine
¼ teaspoon pepper
1 teaspoon salt
¼ cup grated Parmesan cheese

Boil the potatoes in salted water to cover until tender. Mash or rice. While still hot, add the sour cream, cottage cheese, onion, butter or margarine, pepper and salt. Mix well.

Place in a casserole. Sprinkle Parmesan on top. Bake in a 325°F oven for 30 minutes. *Serves 8-10.*

POTATO BACON CASSEROLE

A good buffet dish because you can get it ready in advance and bake it whenever is most convenient.

6 medium potatoes
1 teaspoon salt
⅛ teaspoon pepper
3 tablespoons butter
¼ cup hot milk
⅓ cup chopped onion
⅓ cup chopped green pepper
4 strips bacon
2 eggs
½ cup sharp cheddar cheese, grated

Cook the potatoes in salted water. While the potatoes are cooking, fry the bacon until crisp and cut into small pieces. In 2 tablespoons bacon drippings, cook the onion and green pepper until tender. Place the potatoes, salt, pepper, butter and milk in the large bowl of an electric mixer. Begin beating at low speed and move up gradually to high speed, beating until the potatoes are fluffy. Add the eggs, cheese, onion, green pepper and bacon. Beat until well mixed. Bake in a buttered casserole at 350°F for 30 to 35 minutes.   *Serves 6.*

POTATO PANCAKES

Our version of the classic German potato pancake. Serve with sausage and applesauce for a great lunch.

2 cups grated raw potato (peeled)
3 eggs, beaten
2 tablespoons flour
1 teaspoon salt
1 tablespoon grated onion

Chill the grated potato in ice water; drain and dry well on towel. Add eggs, flour, salt and onion. Shape into patties about 3 inches in diameter. Brown each side until crisp, in ¼ inch hot fat. Serve immediately.   *Serves 4.*

SWISS POTATO SOUFFLE

A pleasant change from the baked potato-mashed potato routine.

> 5 potatoes, baked and riced
> ¼ cup soft butter
> 2 ounces Swiss Gruyère cheese, grated fine
> 2 teaspoons chopped chives
> 1 teaspoon salt
> ⅛ teaspoon pepper
> ⅛ teaspoon savory
> 3 eggs, separated
> 1 cup heavy cream, whipped

Mix the cooled potato with butter, cheese, chives and seasonings. Fold beaten egg yolks into the cream; then fold into the potatoes.

Beat the egg whites until soft peaks form; gently fold into the potato. Spoon into a 1½-quart soufflé dish. Bake in a 350°F oven for 1 hour or until lightly browned on top. Serve at once. *Serves 6.*

BAKED RICE PILAF

The Parmesan makes this unusually tasty.

> 1 cup uncooked, long-grain rice
> 4 tablespoons butter or margarine
> 2 cloves garlic, minced
> 2 cups hot beef or chicken broth
> ½ teaspoon salt
> ¼ cup freshly grated Parmesan cheese

Sauté the garlic and rice in the butter or margarine until golden. Pour into a casserole, add the broth and salt. Cover tightly and bake in a 350°F oven for 25 minutes or until the liquid is absorbed. Add the cheese and stir until cheese is well mixed and the rice is fluffy. *Serves 4.*

SHERRIED BROWN RICE

Growing more popular every day as people become more nutrition-conscious. And brown rice has a flavor that beats that of white rice by a country mile. Serve this recipe with chicken or duck.

> 1 cup long-grain parboiled brown rice*
> 2⅔ cups water
> 1 teaspoon salt
> 1 tablespoon butter
> 1 tablespoon chopped onion
> ½ pound fresh mushrooms, sliced
> ¼ cup sherry

Bring the water to a boil. Add the rice and salt. Cover tightly and cook over low heat until all the water is absorbed (about 50 minutes).

Brown the onions in butter and add the sliced mushrooms. Cook 5 minutes or until the mushrooms are soft. Stir in the sherry and mix well with the rice.

Serves 6.

*If you use rice that is not packaged parboiled (like "Uncle Ben's"), it will take longer to cook.

OVEN BAKED RICE

Here's the best way to cook rice. And please remember to use long-grain *rice, not minute rice.*

> 1½ cups long-grain rice
> 1½ teaspoons salt
> ⅛ teaspoon pepper
> 2 tablespoons butter
> 3½ cups boiling water

Combine and stir all ingredients until the butter is melted. Cover and bake for 45 minutes in a 350°F oven. Do not remove the lid while the rice is in the oven. When done, fluff lightly with fork.

Serves 6.

CRACKED WHEAT PILAF

A nice change from rice and very good for you. Look for bulgur in health food stores and better supermarkets.

1 cup bulgur (cracked wheat)
½ cup chopped onions
6 tablespoons butter or margarine
2 cups beef or chicken stock, boiling
½ teaspoon salt
¼ teaspoon freshly ground black pepper

Sauté dry bulgur in 4 tablespoons of the butter or margarine, stirring, until thoroughly coated. In the remaining butter, sauté the onion separately until soft.

Combine the onion with the bulgur and remaining ingredients in a casserole. Cover and bake 30 minutes in a 350°F oven. Stir gently with a fork. Cover and bake again for an additional 15 minutes.

At the end of the baking time, all the liquid should be absorbed and the bulgur moist but fluffy.   *Serves 4.*

SWEET POTATO PUFFS

6 sweet potatoes
2 tablespoons butter
½ teaspoon salt
2 teaspoons brown sugar
1 tablespoon frozen orange juice concentrate
1 egg
2 tablespoons water
½ cup crushed cornflakes

Leave the sweet potatoes in their jackets, cover with boiling water and keep boiling until tender, about 25 minutes. Rice or mash, then add the next four ingredients and beat with a wire whisk until very light.

Form into balls and dip in a mixture of the egg and water, then roll in crushed cornflakes. Fry in a deep fryer preheated to 380°F until golden brown.   *Serves 6.*

RELISHES
and Other Accompaniments

A relish tray adds extra color and zest to any meal. It will be an extra treat for your guests too, because few people go to the trouble of making up a nice relish tray any more.

There's also a good, practical reason to serve relishes "and other accompaniments." No food tastes the same to all of us, and it could be that the meat or fish you think is just perfect might, in the opinion of some of your guests, "need a little something." It might well be that they'll find that something on the relish tray.

No matter how perfect the roast beef, we must have a touch of hot mustard and horseradish to go with it. Lamb is one of our favorites, but it's nothing without mint sauce.

With a relish tray you will also avoid the embarrassment of having someone ask for the catsup or Worcestershire sauce.

SPICY PEAR CHUTNEY

Serve warm or chilled, with poultry or cold cuts.

8 canned pear halves
1 medium-size onion, chopped
¼ cup seedless raisins
¼ cup honey
2 tablespoons vinegar
¼ teaspoon allspice
¼ teaspoon salt

Combine all the ingredients except the pear halves in a saucepan. Then add the pears and heat to boiling. Simmer, uncovered, for 30 minutes, stirring often.

Makes 1½ cups.

CURRIED FRUIT

We always serve this at brunch on New Year's Day and it's always popular — even with people who are still feeling the effects of the night before.

2 cups canned peach halves, drained
2 cups canned pear halves, drained
2 cups canned pineapple chunks, drained
1 cup seedless sultana raisins
¾ cup light brown sugar
⅓ cup melted butter
2 teaspoons curry powder

Combine the fruits. Blend the sugar and curry powder and mix with the melted butter. Place the fruit in a casserole and pour mixture over. Bake 1 hour at 325°F. Cover and refrigerate overnight.

Heat at 325°F until hot, adding a little fruit juice if it seems dry.

Especially nice when served with sausage or ham.

Makes 8 cups.

BRANDIED PEACHES

Goes with turkey and ham best of all.

> 2 14-ounce cans cling peach halves in
>   heavy syrup
> 1 cup brown sugar
> 1 tablespoon whole cloves
> 1 teaspoon allspice
> ½ cup cider vinegar
> 4 tablespoons brandy

Put the peach halves and syrup, lessened by 4 table-spoonsful, into a saucepan. Add the sugar, cloves, allspice and vinegar. Bring to a boil. Simmer 8 minutes and cool.

Add the brandy. Pierce each peach half with one whole clove. Store in a covered jar in the refrigerator for 24 hours before serving. *Makes 1 quart.*

EASY CHRISTMAS PICKLES

The red and green color combination makes these pickles especially appropriate for the holiday season.

> 4 large dill pickles
> ½ cup canned pimientos, drained
> ⅔ cup vinegar
> ⅓ cup water
> 1 cup sugar

Heat the vinegar, water and sugar to boiling. Slice the dill pickles crosswise. Slice the pimientos. Add to the vinegar mixture. Cover and let stand one week before serving. *Makes 2 cups.*

APPLE RELISH

Try this with fish, ham or roast pork.

> 3 tart apples, medium size
> 3 dill pickles, medium size
> 1 onion, medium size
> ⅓ cup sugar
> ¼ cup vinegar

Halve and core the apples, but do not peel them. Put the apples, pickles and onion through a food chopper, using the coarse blade.

Combine in a small bowl with sugar and vinegar. Chill before serving. *Makes 3 cups.*

CRANBERRY FRUIT RELISH

Goes well with ham, as well as with chicken and turkey.

> 1 orange
> ½ lemon
> 2 cups whole, fresh cranberries
> 1 cup crushed pineapple, drained
> 1 teaspoon curry powder

Quarter and seed the orange and lemon, leaving the rind on. Put through the food chopper with the cranberries. Combine with the other ingredients. Chill overnight. *Makes 2 cups.*

GREEN PEPPER RELISH

Can be served with all cold meats.

> 2 pounds sweet green peppers
> 1 pound tomatoes, peeled and diced

1 pound onions,
  peeled and sliced
¼ cup olive oil
1 teaspoon salt
¾ cup wine vinegar

Remove stems and seeds from the peppers. Slice the peppers lengthwise. Place the peppers, tomatoes, onions, olive oil and salt in a saucepan. Cover and simmer 1 hour, stirring from time to time.

Add the vinegar and continue to simmer, uncovered, until most of the liquid has evaporated. Cool and place in covered bowl or jar. Refrigerate for two days before using.   *Makes 1¾ cups.*

INDIAN CORN RELISH

We seem to serve this more during the fall than any other time of year. Harvest influence, probably, though we've never made it with fresh corn.

1 small onion
½ cup vinegar
3 tablespoons sugar
1 tablespoon mustard seed
¼ teaspoon salt
¼ teaspoon celery seed
¼ teaspoon dry mustard
1 12-ounce can Mexican-style whole-
  kernel corn, drained.

Slice the onion paper thin. Add the vinegar, sugar, mustard seed, salt, celery seed and dry mustard. Place in a saucepan and bring to boil. Simmer 5 minutes. Remove from heat. Add the corn. Cool.   *Makes 1¾ cups.*

CUMBERLAND SAUCE

Goes particularly well with duck and venison.

1 cup currant jelly
1 tablespoon prepared mustard
1 teaspoon grated onion
½ teaspoon ginger
grated peel of 1 orange and 1 lemon
½ cup orange juice
2 tablespoons lemon juice
½ cup Marsala wine
1 tablespoon cornstarch
2 tablespoons water

In a saucepan, combine all the ingredients except the cornstarch and water. Mix well and cook over hot water or very low heat, stirring, until the jelly melts. Mix the cornstarch and water, add to the sauce and stir until the sauce is thickened and transparent. *Makes about 2½ cups.*

CREAMY MUSTARD SAUCE

A nice way to add zest to cold meats.

1 cup sour cream
1 tablespoon fresh lemon juice
2 tablespoons dry mustard
½ teaspoon salt
½ teaspoon sugar

Blend all the ingredients well. Chill before serving.
Makes 1 cup.

BREADS, BISCUITS, DOUGHNUTS, PANCAKES, MUFFINS AND ROLLS

Everybody knows the importance of eating a good breakfast. Next to getting out of the right side of the bed, there's no better way to start the day happy. And almost any item in this category will help you do *that* much better than the conventional piece of toast.

At lunch, try some of the quick breads. Different, delicious and inspirational.

At dinner, add an assortment to the bread basket, especially if you're in the habit of serving the same old bread or rolls day after day, night after night. (Restaurants please note!)

"WHAT'S IN THE OVEN?"

If you want to realize a feeling of real accomplishment, learn to bake. A psychology professor tells us that the whole process has deep religious overtones. Perhaps. All we know is that baking is fun and nothing smells as good or tastes as good as something right out of the oven.

Anything you bake at home will be better and cheaper than store-bought. And there's not one item in the most fancy "Patisserie" you couldn't learn to make at home. Yet many good cooks and many professional chefs do not — or will not — bake for themselves. Guess it's because baked goods are so easy to buy.

Everybody should learn to bake *something* from scratch just for his or her own satisfaction, and bread is one of the most rewarding. The man or woman who is known to bake good bread is held in high esteem.

The baking of bread can be a complicated, drawn-out process or it can be comparatively simple. Our recipe for Irish Whole Wheat Bread belongs in the latter category, and we urge you to give it a try.

WHEAT GERM BISCUITS

The wheat germ makes them better — and different.

1½ cups unsifted all-purpose flour
½ cup regular wheat germ
3 teaspoons baking powder
1 teaspoon salt
¼ cup shortening
¾ cup light cream

Combine the flour, wheat germ, baking powder and salt in a bowl. Stir well to blend. Cut in the shortening until the mixture resembles coarse meal. Add the cream and stir with a fork until all ingredients are moistened.

Turn out on to a lightly floured board and knead gently 20 times. Roll the dough to ½-inch thickness and cut with a floured 2-inch biscuit cutter. Bake on an ungreased baking sheet at 450°F for 8 to 10 minutes. *Makes 12 biscuits.*

BANANA BREAD

So good that it's worth letting your bananas go mushy on purpose.

1¾ cups sifted all-purpose flour
2 teaspoons baking powder
¼ teaspoon baking soda
½ teaspoon salt
⅓ cup butter
¾ cup sugar
2 eggs, well beaten
1 cup mashed, fully ripe bananas

Sift together the flour, baking powder, soda and salt. Cream the butter. Add the sugar gradually and continue beating until light and fluffy. Add the eggs and beat well.

Add the flour mixture alternately with the mashed bananas a little at a time, mixing after each addition only enough to moisten the dry ingredients.

Turn into a greased loaf pan (8½x4½x2½ inches) and bake in a 350°F oven for 1 hour and 10 minutes.

Makes 1 loaf.

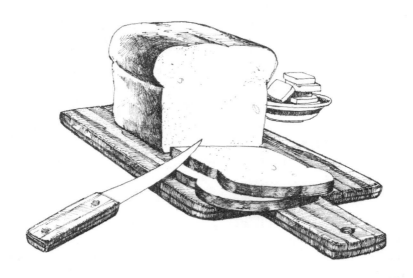

BEER BREAD

A coarse-textured bread that goes well with salads and cheese.

>   3 cups self-rising flour
>   ½ teaspoon salt
>   ½ cup all-bran cereal
>   2 eggs, well beaten
>   2 teaspoons honey
>   6 tablespoons butter or margarine,
>   melted
>   1 12-ounce can beer, at room
>   temperature

Mix the flour, salt and cereal. Add the eggs, honey and butter or margarine. Mix well and then add the beer. Beat and put into a well-greased, floured 9½x5½x3-inch loaf pan. Bake 35 to 45 minutes, or until brown in a 475°F oven.

Makes 1 loaf.

IRISH WHOLE WHEAT BREAD

As we mentioned before, baking bread is good for the soul.
This is a good one to learn on.

> 2 packages active dry yeast
> ⅔ cup lukewarm water
> 5 cups whole wheat flour
> 1 tablespoon honey
> 3 tablespoons molasses
> ⅔ cup lukewarm water
> 1 tablespoon salt
> ⅓ cup wheat germ
> 1⅓ cups lukewarm water
> 1 tablespoon melted butter

Sprinkle the yeast over the first ⅔ cup lukewarm water and add the honey. Set aside for a few minutes while preparing the dough. Whole wheat flour should be warmed in a 250°F oven for about 20 minutes before using.

Combine the molasses with the second ⅔ cup lukewarm water. Combine the yeast and molasses mixtures. Stir into the flour, add the salt and wheat germ, then the 1⅓ cups lukewarm water.

Grease a large loaf pan (9x5x3 inches). Turn dough into pan, smoothing the top. Let rise for 60 minutes in a warm, draft-free spot.

Preheat the oven to 375°F. Bake the bread for 55 minutes or until the top is nicely browned. Remove from the oven, pour melted butter over the top and cool on a rack for 10 minutes.

Loosen the loaf, turn out on to a rack and cool completely before slicing. *Makes 1 2-pound loaf.*

LEMON TEA BREAD

You can really taste the lemon in this. Be prepared to hand out the recipe every time you serve it.

½ cup butter
1 cup sugar
grated rind of 1 lemon
2 eggs, beaten
1½ cups all-purpose flour
1 teaspoon baking powder
½ cup milk
½ cup walnuts, chopped

Cream the butter, and add the sugar and grated lemon rind. Add the eggs. Sift together the flour and baking powder and add alternately with the milk. Add the chopped walnuts. Bake in a greased loaf pan in a 375°F oven for 35 minutes.

As soon as the bread is removed from the oven, pour over the surface a mixture of:

¼ cup sugar
juice and grated rind of 1 large lemon

Let cool for 10 minutes before removing from pan.

Makes 1 loaf.

OATMEAL BREAKFAST MUFFINS

We have a sentimental attachment for these muffins. They were the first we ever made after we went into the the inn business. We still make them — and they're still a success.

> ¾ cup sifted all-purpose flour
> 2 teaspoons baking powder
> ¾ teaspoon salt
> ⅓ cup sugar
> 1 cup quick-cooking oats
> ¼ cup butter or margarine
> 2 eggs, lightly beaten
> ½ cup milk
> 1 tablespoon melted butter or margarine
> ¼ cup quick-cooking oats

Sift the flour, baking powder, salt and sugar together. Stir in the 1 cup of oats. Cut in the butter or margarine with a pastry blender. Combine the eggs and milk and add to the dry ingredients, mixing lightly with a fork. Mix only until the ingredients are moistened. Half fill 12 well-greased muffin pan cups. Mix the melted butter or margarine with the ¼ cup of oats. Sprinkle evenly over the muffins. Bake at 400°F for 20-25 minutes.

(When ready for the oven, these muffins may be covered with waxed paper and stored in the refrigerator overnight, to be baked the following morning.)

Makes 12 muffins.

ORANGE BRAN BREAD

A very old recipe that's come into its own in recent years due to the growing interest in fiber foods.

> 1 cup whole bran
> ¾ cup orange juice
> ½ cup milk
> 2 cups sifted all-purpose flour

½ cup sugar
3 teaspoons baking powder
¼ teaspoon baking soda
1 teaspoon salt
grated rind of ½ orange
1 egg, well beaten
¼ cup melted shortening

Combine the bran, orange juice and milk. Let stand 15 minutes. Sift together the flour, sugar, baking powder, soda and salt.

Combine the grated orange rind, beaten egg and melted shortening and add to the bran mixture. Then add the sifted dry ingredients, mixing only until blended.

Turn into a greased loaf pan (9x5 inches) and bake in a 325°F oven for 1 hour and 15 minutes. *Makes 1 loaf.*

QUICK BROWN BREAD

A traditional New England bread that is especially good with chicken, ham, and baked beans. Hard to go wrong making this.

2 cups whole wheat flour
1 teaspoon salt
½ teaspoon soda
1½ teaspoons baking powder
1 egg
1 cup buttermilk
½ cup molasses
¼ cup shortening

Mix the flour, salt, soda and baking powder thoroughly. Beat the egg and add to it the buttermilk, molasses and shortening. Add the liquid to the dry ingredients and stir only enough to barely mix. Bake in a well-greased loaf pan at 350°F for 30 minutes.

Cut in slices and serve hot. *Makes 1 loaf.*

SHREDDED WHEAT BREAD

A master baker's favorite recipe. Makes a light, delicious bread that's especially good for sandwiches.

2 large shredded wheat biscuits, crumbled
2 cups boiling water
1 teaspoon salt
⅔ cup molasses
3 tablespoons butter
½ cup lukewarm water
1 cake compressed yeast
5 to 6 cups all-purpose flour

Pour boiling water over the shredded wheat. Add the molasses, salt and butter. Let cool to lukewarm. Add the yeast, dissolved in the lukewarm water. Mix together thoroughly. Add flour gradually until the mixture forms a firm dough.

Turn out on to a lightly floured board. Cover and let stand for 10 minutes, then knead the dough until smooth. Place in a greased bowl, turning to grease the top of the dough. Cover. Let rise in a warm place until doubled in bulk (about 1 hour).

Punch down the dough. Divide in half; shape into two loaves. Place each one in a greased 8½x4½x2½-inch loaf pan. Cover and let rise until doubled in bulk (about 50 minutes).

Bake in a 325°F oven for 50 minutes or until the loaves sound hollow when tapped. Turn out of the pans on to a wire rack. *Makes 2 loaves.*

WHOLE WHEAT HONEY BREAD

Rich and wholesome — the kind of bread that warms the heart of the health food fan.

8 to 8½ cups unsifted stone-ground whole wheat flour
4 teaspoons salt
2 packages active dry yeast
1½ cups milk
1½ cups water
⅓ cup honey
6 tablespoons butter

In a large mixing bowl, thoroughly stir together 3 cups of the whole wheat flour, the salt and undissolved yeast.

Place the milk, water, honey and butter in a small saucepan over low heat until warm (130°F). Gradually stir the liquid into the flour mixture and beat for 2 minutes at medium speed of the electric mixer, scraping the bowl occasionally. Add 1 cup flour. Beat at high speed for 2 minutes. Stir in enough additional flour to make a stiff dough.

Turn out on to a lightly floured board; cover and let stand for 10 minutes. Knead the dough until smooth and elastic.

Place in a greased bowl, turning the dough to grease top. Cover. Let rise in a warm place until doubled in bulk (50-60 minutes).

Punch down the dough. Divide in half; shape into two loaves. Place each loaf in a greased 8½x4½x2½-inch loaf pan. Cover. Let rise again until doubled in bulk (about 50 minutes).

Bake in a 375°F oven for about 35 minutes. When the bread is done, the loaves will sound hollow when tapped. Turn out of the pans on to a wire rack. *Makes 2 loaves.*

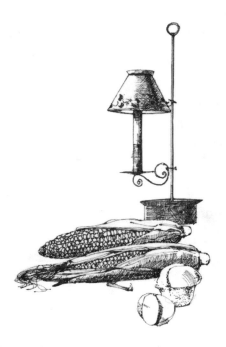

CRANBERRY MUFFINS

The only people who don't like these muffins are those who don't like cranberries.

¼ cup shortening
¼ cup sugar
1 egg, unbeaten
½ teaspoon salt
2 cups all-purpose flour
5 teaspoons baking powder
1 cup milk
1 cup cranberries, coarsely chopped
1 teaspoon grated orange rind

Cream the sugar and shortening together. Add the egg. Sift together the salt, flour and baking powder, and add to the creamed mixture alternately with the milk. Fold the cranberries and orange rind into the batter. Mix for 10 to 20 seconds only.

Fill well-greased muffin pan cups about two-thirds full and bake at 425°F for 20 minutes. *Makes 12 large muffins.*

BUTTERMILK PANCAKES

If you want to overwhelm your guests at breakfast some morning, just casually ask them: "What kind of pancakes would you like? Buttermilk? Banana? Apple? Blueberry?"

Use the recipe below as is for *Buttermilk Pancakes*. For *Apple Pancakes* add to the batter before baking 1½ cups grated apple, 1 tablespoon lemon juice, and 1 tablespoon sugar; for *Banana Pancakes,* add 1 cup mashed ripe bananas, 1 tablespoon lemon juice and 1 tablespoon sugar; for *Blueberry Pancakes* add 1 tablespoon sugar and fold in 1 cup fresh blueberries.

> 2 eggs
> 1½ cups buttermilk
> 3 tablespoons butter, melted
> 1½ cups all-purpose flour
> 1 tablespoon sugar
> 1½ teaspoons baking powder
> ½ teaspoon soda
> ½ teaspoon salt

Beat the eggs; add the remaining ingredients and beat with a rotary beater until smooth. Grease a heated griddle. To test, sprinkle with water. If drops jump around, the griddle is ready. Pour batter from a large spoon. Turn the pancakes when puffed and full of bubbles. Bake the other side until golden brown. *Makes 14 4-inch pancakes.*

CORNMEAL PANCAKES

Worth getting up a few minutes earlier to make.

    1 cup enriched yellow cornmeal
    ½ teaspoon salt
    1 cup boiling water
    2 tablespoons melted butter or
      margarine
    1 cup buttermilk
    1 egg, slightly beaten
    ¼ cup all-purpose flour
    ¼ teaspoon baking soda

Combine the cornmeal and salt. Slowly stir in the boiling water and melted butter. Cover and let stand for 10 minutes. Stir in the buttermilk and egg. Combine the flour and baking soda and stir quickly into the batter. The batter will be very thin.

Bake on a well-greased griddle over medium heat, using a tablespoon of batter for each griddle cake. Stir the batter often and keep the griddle well greased. When golden brown underneath, turn to brown the other side. Turn only once.

Serve with warmed maple syrup.

Makes 3½ dozen small, thin cakes.

GOLDEN PUFFS

Try these freshly made with your morning coffee. A great way to start the day.

    2½ cups sifted all-purpose flour
    ¼ cup sugar
    3 teaspoons baking powder
    1 teaspoon salt

1 teaspoon mace
¼ cup corn oil
¾ cup milk
1 egg, beaten

Sift the flour, sugar, baking powder, salt and mace together, then add the oil, milk and beaten egg. Stir with a fork until thoroughly mixed.

Drop by teaspoonsful into deep hot oil or fat at 375°F. Fry until golden brown — about 3 minutes. Drain on absorbent paper. Roll the warm puffs in sugar.

Makes 2½ dozen.

PINEAPPLE MUFFINS

Friends in the catering business claim this is the most popular muffin they serve. We believe it.

½ cup sugar
⅓ cup shortening
⅓ cup honey
2 eggs
1⅓ cups all-bran
1⅓ cups all-purpose flour
2 teaspoons soda
½ teaspoon salt
1 cup evaporated milk
1 cup crushed pineapple, well drained

Cream the sugar, shortening and honey together, then add to this mixture the remaining ingredients and mix lightly. Fill greased muffin pan cups two-thirds full. Bake for 25 minutes in a 350°F oven. (Or cover the pans with wax paper and store in the refrigerator overnight to bake up fresh in the morning.) *Makes 18 muffins.*

ONE HOUR YEAST ROLLS

A quick, easy version of the famous Parker House Roll.

2 packages active dry yeast
¼ cup lukewarm water
1¼ cups milk
3 tablespoons sugar
2 tablespoons butter
¾ teaspoon salt
4 cups sifted all-purpose flour

Dissolve the yeast in the lukewarm water. Place the milk, sugar, butter and salt in a pan. Heat until lukewarm. Add the yeast and flour and mix well. Place in a greased bowl and brush the top with melted butter. Let rise for 15 minutes.

Turn out on to a floured board. Pat until ¾ inch thick. Cut into rounds with a floured biscuit cutter. Fold the rolls over and press the edges together lightly. Place on a greased baking sheet. Let rise for 15 minutes.

Bake in a 425°F oven for 10 minutes. Brush with melted butter. *Makes about 3 dozen rolls.*

SCOTTISH OATMEAL SCONES

Must be served warm. Very good with strawberry or raspberry jam.

1¼ cups sifted all-purpose flour
⅓ cup sugar
2 teaspoons baking powder
½ teaspoon salt
¼ cup shortening
¼ cup butter
1 cup quick-cooking oats
¼ cup raisins or currants
⅓ cup milk
1 tablespoon melted butter

Sift together the flour, sugar, baking powder and salt into a bowl. Cut in the shortening and butter until the mixture resembles coarse crumbs. Mix in the oats and raisins or currants. Add the milk, mixing just until the dry ingredients are moistened.

Turn the dough out on to a lightly floured surface; knead gently five or six times. Roll to form a 7-inch circle. Brush the top of the dough with melted butter. Cut into six pie-shaped wedges. Bake on an ungreased cookie sheet in a preheated 375°F oven for about 15 minutes, or until lightly browned. *Makes 6 scones.*

PIES

While there are many good-looking, good-tasting commercial cakes, cookies, breads and rolls on the market, there are precious few store-bought pies worth eating. Some of the best looking taste the worst. There are exceptions of course, and there are probably many small bakeshops nestled around the country presided over by an apple-cheeked baker who turns out superb pies. If there's one near you, count your blessings.

A wholesome, delicious, fresh pie is something modern science has yet to learn how to produce in quantity. Existing attempts are sad, indeed. Generally speaking, if you like good pie, you've got to make your own. And why not? Pies are no more difficult to make than anything else. Worth it, even if they were.

When whoever-it-was said: "The way to a man's heart is through his stomach," a juicy wedge of fresh apple or blueberry pie was surely the vehicle he had in mind.

SPECIAL PIE CRUST

Should always be good if worked with a quick, light touch.

> 2 cups all-purpose flour
> ½ teaspoon salt
> ¼ teaspoon baking powder
> ⅔ cup vegetable shortening or lard
> ⅓ cup ice water

Sift together the flour, salt and baking powder and cut in lard or vegetable shortening until the mixture resembles coarse meal. Add the water all at once, and press the dough lightly until it just holds together. Roll into a ball. Wrap the dough in foil and chill until ready to use.

When ready to roll the dough, place on a lightly floured board. The dough should be soft enough not to break when it is rolled; it should be stiff enough not to stick to a lightly floured board. Roll from the center outward with an even pressure, to a thickness of ⅛ inch.

Makes a 9-inch 2-crust pie or two 9-inch pie shells.

APPLESAUCE CRUMB PIE

A traditional New England recipe.

> 2 cups unsweetened applesauce
> 1 cup light brown sugar
> 3 tablespoons butter or margarine
> 1 cup sultana raisins
> 4 eggs
> ½ cup all-purpose flour
> ¼ cup sugar
> ½ teaspoon ginger
> ¼ teaspoon nutmeg
> 2 tablespoons butter or margarine
> 1 cup heavy cream, whipped
> 1 9-inch unbaked pie shell with high
> fluted edge

Place the applesauce and brown sugar in a saucepan. Bring to a boil, reduce the heat and simmer for 20 minutes, stirring occasionally. Remove from heat; add 3 tablespoons butter or margarine and stir until melted. Stir in the raisins. Cool.

In a small mixing bowl, beat the eggs and add to the applesauce mixture. Pour into the pie shell. Bake in a 375°F oven on the low rack for 20 minutes. Remove from the oven.

Blend the flour, sugar and spices and cut in the 2 tablespoons butter or margarine until crumbly. Sprinkle evenly over the top of the pie and continue baking until the top and crust are golden brown (about 25 minutes).

Serve with unsweetened whipped cream.

BAKED ALASKA PIE

A very easy pie to make that will keep a month in the freezer.

> 1 9-inch pie shell, baked until golden brown and cooled
> 1 pint lime sherbet or pistachio ice cream, softened
> 1 pint vanilla ice cream, softened
> 1 pint strawberry ice cream, softened
> 3 egg whites
> 1 teaspoon cream of tartar
> 6 tablespoons sugar

Spoon alternate spoonsful of sherbet and ice creams into the pie shell; pack down firmly and level the top. Freeze until very hard.

Beat the egg whites until frothy, then add the cream of tartar and beat until soft peaks form. Add the sugar, one tablespoon at a time, beating until stiff, glossy peaks form. Mound quickly on to the pie, spreading to seal all edges. Bake in a 425°F oven 3 or 4 minutes or until lightly browned. Serve immediately or freeze.

Want to gild the lily? When serving, dribble a little chocolate sauce over the pie, or garnish the top with crushed and sweetened fresh strawberries.

GLAZED BLUEBERRY PIE

The combination of fresh and cooked blueberries gives this pie a unique, fresh flavor.

    4 cups hulled fresh blueberries
    1 cup sugar
    3 tablespoons cornstarch
    1 tablespoon lemon juice
    1 tablespoon confectioners' sugar
    1 cup heavy cream, whipped
    1 tablespoon sugar
    1 9-inch baked pie shell

Crush 2 cups of berries and blend with the sugar and cornstarch, which have been mixed together. Cook over direct heat, stirring frequently, until thick and smooth (8 to 10 minutes). Add the lemon juice. Cool. Then fold the remaining fresh berries into the mixture.

Sprinkle the confectioners' sugar over the bottom of the pie shell and add the filling. Chill in the refrigerator for 2 hours. Serve topped with the whipped cream sweetened with the 1 tablespoon sugar.

BRANDY ALEXANDER PIE

Light, refreshing and extremely *popular!*

> 1 envelope unflavored gelatin
> ½ cup cold water
> ⅔ cup sugar
> ⅛ teaspoon salt
> 2 eggs, separated
> ¼ cup cognac
> ¼ cup crème de cacao
> 2 cups heavy cream, whipped
> 1 9-inch Chocolate Crumb Crust (see below)

Sprinkle the gelatin over cold water in saucepan. Add ⅓ cup of the sugar, salt, and the egg yolks. Stir to blend. Heat over low heat while stirring until the gelatin dissolves and mixture thickens.

Remove from the heat and stir in the cognac and crème de cacao. Chill until the mixture starts to mound slightly.

Beat the egg whites until stiff. Gradually beat in the remaining sugar and fold into the thickened gelatin mixture. Fold in one cup of the whipped cream. Turn into the crust. Chill. Top with the remaining cup of whipped cream.

CHOCOLATE CRUMB CRUST

> 1½ cups chocolate wafer crumbs, crushed very fine
> 6 tablespoons melted butter

Mix well and pat firmly into a 9-inch pan, covering bottom and sides. Either chill thoroughly before filling or bake in a 300°F oven for 15 minutes.

FRENCH SILK PIE

This is the best chocolate pie we've ever tasted.

½ cup butter
¾ cup sugar
1 square unsweetened chocolate
1 teaspoon vanilla
2 eggs
1 cup heavy cream, whipped
1 tablespoon crème de cacao
1 9-inch Meringue Pie Shell

Beat softened butter in the electric mixer until fluffy. Add the sugar gradually and beat until smooth. Melt the chocolate over hot water and add with vanilla to the creamed mixture. Beat in. Add the eggs, one at a time, beating 4 minutes each time.

Pour this mixture into Meringue Pie Shell (see below) and top with whipped cream flavored with crème de cacao.

MERINGUE PIE SHELL

3 egg whites
pinch salt
¼ teaspoon cream of tartar
½ teaspoon vanilla
¾ cup sugar
⅓ cup finely chopped walnuts

Combine the egg whites, salt and cream of tartar and beat to a stiff foam. Beat in the vanilla. Add the sugar gradually, beating until peaks are formed and the sugar is dissolved.

Spread in a well-greased 9-inch pie tin. Build up the sides; sprinkle the bottom with chopped nuts. Bake in a 275°F oven for 1 hour. Cool and fill.

CHOCOLATE BROWNIE PIE

Probably addictive. The owner of the little bakeshop who gave us this recipe ate it for breakfast.

> 2 squares unsweetened chocolate
> 2 tablespoons butter or margarine
> 3 large eggs
> ½ cup sugar
> ¾ cup dark corn syrup
> ¾ cup pecan halves
> 1 9-inch unbaked pie shell

Melt the unsweetened chocolate and butter or margarine over hot water. Then beat together the eggs, sugar, chocolate mixture and corn syrup. Stir in the pecan halves.

Pour into the unbaked pie shell. Bake 40 to 50 minutes in a 375°F oven or just until set. Serve warm or cold with ice cream or whipped cream.

LEMON-LIME SKYSCRAPER PIE

Light, refreshing, and pretty to look at.

- 1 envelope unflavored gelatin
- 1¼ cups sugar, divided
- ¼ teaspoon salt
- 6 eggs, separated
- ⅓ cup water
- ⅓ cup lemon juice
- ⅓ cup lime juice
- 1 teaspoon grated lemon rind
- 1 teaspoon grated lime rind
- ½ teaspoon cream of tartar
- 1 9-inch baked pie shell

Mix together the gelatin, ½ cup sugar and the salt in the top of the double boiler. Beat the egg yolks with the water, lemon and lime juices; stir into the gelatin mixture. Place over boiling water and cook, stirring constantly, until the gelatin dissolves and the mixture thickens slightly (about 6 minutes). Add both rinds. Chill, stirring occasionally, until the mixture mounds slightly when dropped from a spoon.

Beat the egg whites with the cream of tartar until stiff but not dry; then gradually add the remaining ¾ cup sugar and beat until very stiff. Fold in the gelatin mixture. If necessary, chill until the mixture will pile. Turn into the pie shell, piling high in center. Chill until firm.

OATMEAL PIE

A little like pecan pie, but cakier.

- 3 tablespoons butter or margarine
- 5 tablespoons packed light brown sugar

2½ tablespoons rolled oats
1½ cups light corn syrup
1 teaspoon salt
3 eggs, separated
1 cup pitted dates, chopped
1 cup walnuts, chopped
1 9-inch unbaked pie shell
1 cup heavy cream, whipped

Cream together the butter or margarine, brown sugar and rolled oats. Add the corn syrup, salt and beaten egg yolks. Blend the mixture well. Stir in the dates and walnuts. Fold in the egg whites, stiffly beaten, and spoon the mixture into the unbaked pastry shell. Bake at 325°F for 55 minutes.

Serve chilled with unsweetened whipped cream.

RHUBARB CUSTARD PIE

Should be made only with fresh rhubarb, in season.

2 cups rhubarb, diced
1 cup sugar
2 eggs, separated
1 cup milk
2 tablespoons flour
¼ teaspoon salt
1 teaspoon lemon juice
¼ cup sugar
1 9-inch unbaked pie shell

Stew the rhubarb with ¾ cup sugar, in water just to cover, until soft. Cool. Add the milk and the yolks of the eggs beaten with ¼ cup sugar, flour and salt.

Add the lemon juice. Pour into the unbaked pie shell. Flute a rim to stand up above the pie plate. Bake in a 450°F oven for 10 minutes, then in a 325°F oven for 25 minutes.

Beat the egg whites until stiff, adding the remaining ¼ cup sugar gradually. Beat until glossy. Spread the meringue on the pie and return to a 300°F oven for 10 minutes or until the meringue is slightly browned.

VERMONT PECAN PIE

The maple syrup makes it a delicious change-of-pace from the Southern version.

  ⅓ cup butter or margarine
  ½ cup sugar
  ½ cup light corn syrup
  ½ cup maple syrup
  3 eggs, well beaten
  1¼ cups broken pecans
  ¼ teaspoon salt
  ¼ teaspoon vanilla
  1 9-inch unbaked pie shell
  1 cup heavy cream, whipped

Cream the butter or margarine, add the sugar and continue creaming while adding the combined syrups. Blend all thoroughly, then beat in the eggs, nuts, salt and vanilla. Turn into the pie shell and bake for 10 minutes at 450°F, then for 40 to 50 minutes at 325°F.

Serve with unsweetened whipped cream.

CAKES

Why go to all the trouble of baking a cake from scratch when there are so many good mixes on the market? Well, we'll tell you why . . .

Home-baked cakes are better for you because they can contain better ingredients. And home-baked cakes are free from the preservatives and other chemicals almost always found in commercial products. Read the labels on the packages. If *that* doesn't convince you to bake at home, nothing will.

CHEESE CAKE

In our humble opinion, this is the most luscious cheese cake ever created. Actually it's more of a pie than a cake, with a smooth, velvety filling that's wicked rich. Be sure to chill for 12 hours before serving or it won't cut properly.

CRUST

1½ cups graham cracker crumbs
4 tablespoons ground unblanched almonds
6 tablespoons sugar
¼ cup coffee cream
½ cup melted butter

Mix together and press into bottom of a 10-inch spring-form pan.

FILLING

4 eggs
1 cup sugar
1½ tablespoons brandy
3 8-ounce packages cream cheese
1 pint sour cream
2 tablespoons sugar

Beat the eggs, 1 cup sugar, the brandy and cheese together for 20 minutes with the electric mixer. Pour over the crust in the pan and bake 30 minutes at 350°F. Cool for 15 minutes.

Mix the sour cream with 2 tablespoons sugar, spread over the cake and return to the oven. Bake 10 minutes at 350°F.

SAUCE

2 cups fresh or frozen blueberries
⅔ cup sugar
½ cup water
1 tablespoon lemon juice
1 teaspoon cornstarch
⅓ cup water

Heat the blueberries with the sugar, lemon juice and ½

cup water. Bring to a boil and let boil for 3 minutes. If too watery, let the berries cook another 3 to 4 minutes (depends on how much moisture is in the fruit). Dissolve the cornstarch in ⅓ cup cold water; add to the berries and let boil another minute.

Serve warm or cold with Cheese Cake.

CHOCOLATE DATE CAKE

Stays moist until the last crumb is consumed, which doesn't usually take very long.

1 cup pitted dates, chopped
1 teaspoon soda
1½ cups boiling water
¾ cup butter or margarine
1 cup sugar
1 egg
2 cups all-purpose flour
2 teaspoons baking powder
½ teaspoon salt
½ cup sugar
½ cup chopped walnuts
1 6-ounce package semisweet chocolate morsels

In a small bowl combine the dates with the soda and boiling water. In another bowl, cream together the butter and the first cup of sugar. Add the egg and beat until light. Sift the flour, measure, and sift again with the baking powder and salt. Add to the creamed mixture alternately with the date mixture.

Pour the batter into a greased baking pan (13x9 inches). Combine the ½ cup sugar with the walnuts and chocolate morsels; sprinkle evenly over the top of the cake.

Bake in a 350°F oven for 1 hour, or until the cake starts to shrink away from the sides of the pan. Serve warm or cool, with or without whipped cream.

CHOCOLATE MOUSSE CAKE

The best French chef we ever worked with gave us this recipe.

> 12 ounces semisweet chocolate morsels
> 3 tablespoons water
> 3 tablespoons confectioners' sugar
> 7 eggs, separated
> 1 teaspoon vanilla
> 24 ladyfingers (page 182)
> 3 tablespoons light rum
> 2 cups heavy cream, whipped
> ½ square unsweetened chocolate curls

Melt chocolate morsels with water in a double boiler. Add the sugar and mix well; cool slightly. Add the egg yolks and mix well. Cool slightly. Add the vanilla. Beat the egg whites until stiff and fold into the mixture.

Line the sides and bottom of a 9x5x2¾-inch loaf pan with transparent wrap. Place a row of ladyfingers (unsplit), very close together, along the bottom of the pan. Sprinkle with ⅓ of the rum and pour on half of the chocolate mixture. Repeat. Finish with a third layer of ladyfingers sprinkled with rum. Chill for 24 hours.

To serve, turn upside down on a chilled platter; remove the plastic wrap carefully. Cover the sides and top with whipped cream. Spread the top with chocolate curls. Serve in slices. *Serves 10.*

CHOCOLATE-PECAN FRUITCAKE

Like most good fruitcakes, this one will keep for weeks.

> 2 cups sifted all-purpose flour
> 1½ cups sugar
> ½ cup unsweetened cocoa
> 1 teaspoon baking soda
> 1 teaspoon salt
> 1½ cups pecans, coarsely chopped
> 2 cups diced mixed candied fruit

1 cup raisins
1 cup chopped pitted dates
2 eggs
1 cup sour cream
1 teaspoon vanilla
¼ cup melted butter or margarine

Sift together the flour, sugar, cocoa, baking soda and salt. Set aside. Mix together the pecans, candied fruit, raisins and dates.

In a large mixing bowl beat together the eggs, sour cream and vanilla. Add the butter or margarine and then the flour mixture. Beat with the electric mixer at medium speed for 1 minute or by hand until well blended. Add the pecan-fruit mixture and fold in until well distributed. Turn into a generously greased 9-inch tube pan.

Place a shallow pan of hot water on the bottom of the oven. Bake the cake at 300°F for 1¾ hours, or until cake tester comes out clean. Cool in the pan on a wire rack for 10 minutes.

Wrap tightly in plastic or foil and refrigerate for at least a week before serving.

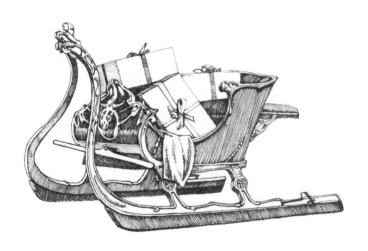

CHOCOLATE REFRIGERATOR CAKE

We could be wrong, but we can't remember ever *serving this cake and not being asked for the recipe, which happens to be a very easy one.*

> 1　egg, separated
> ¼　teaspoon salt
> ½　pint whipping cream
> 1　cup chocolate syrup
> 2　8-inch rounds of sponge or angel cake

Whip the egg yolk with a fork and add salt. Beat the egg white until very stiff. Whip the cream. Place the egg yolk, whipped cream and syrup into a bowl and blend. Fold in the beaten white.

Split the cake rounds to obtain four layers. Spread the above mixture between the layers and on the top and sides. Set in the refrigerator for approximately 24 hours. Serve in wedges.

GOLDEN GLOW CAKE

The orange-chocolate combination gives this old English recipe a very distinguished flavor. Not the easiest cake to make but well worth the effort.

> ½　cup butter
> 1½　cups sugar
> grated rind of ½ orange
> 1　egg, separated
> 1　egg yolk
> 2½　cups all-purpose flour
> ¼　teaspoon salt

4 teaspoons baking powder
1 cup milk
1½ squares unsweetened chocolate,
    melted

Cream the butter and add to it the sugar and grated rind. Add the beaten egg yolks. Sift together the flour, salt, and baking powder. Add the dry ingredients alternately with the milk to the creamed mixture. Fold in the egg white, beaten until stiff.

Divide the batter in two, and to one part add the melted chocolate.

Put by tablespoonsful — alternating dark and light batter — into three greased and lightly floured 10-inch cake pans. Bake in a 375°F oven for 20 to 25 minutes, or until the cake springs back when lightly touched in the center.

Cool in the pans for 10 minutes, then turn out on racks. Fill and frost with the following recipe:

ICING AND FILLING

3 tablespoons melted butter
3 cups confectioners' sugar
2 tablespoons orange juice
grated rind of ½ orange
pulp of 1 orange
1 egg white
3 squares unsweetened chocolate

Put the butter, sugar, orange juice and rind in bowl. Add the seeded orange pulp. Beat all together until smooth. Fold in the stiffly beaten egg white. Spread this icing on the layer being used for the top of the cake.

While the icing is soft, sprinkle the top iced layer with finely shaved unsweetened chocolate, using ½ square.

To the remaining icing add 2½ squares chocolate, melted over hot water. Spread this icing thickly between the layers and on the sides of the cake.

LADYFINGERS

With a supply of these on hand, you'll always have the makings of an elegant dessert.

⅓ cup sifted cake flour
⅓ cup sifted confectioners' sugar
1 whole egg
2 egg yolks
2 egg whites
¼ teaspoon vanilla

Beat the whole egg and 2 yolks until thick and lemon-colored. Whip the whites until stiff, but not dry. Fold the sugar gradually into the whites. Beat until the whites stiffen again. Fold in the egg and yolk mixture and vanilla. Sift the cake flour three times and fold in.

Shape the batter into ovals about 4½ inches long and 1¼ inches wide by putting it through a cookie press. Place on ungreased brown paper cut to fit a cookie sheet. Bake in a 300°F oven for 18 minutes or until pale gold in color.

Makes 24 ladyfingers.

ENGLISH LEMON CURD

Use as a filling for small tarts or any white layer cake. When you feel you deserve a special treat some morning, try it on toast.

1 cup butter
1½ cups sugar
grated rind of 2 lemons
½ cup fresh lemon juice
5 eggs, beaten

Put all the ingredients in the top part of a double boiler over hot (not boiling) water. Cook, stirring constantly, until nearly thick. Cover and continue cooking for 10 minutes. Cool and store in the refrigerator in a covered jar.

Makes 3 cups.

MACAROON CAKE

The unusual feature of this recipe is that the coconut mixture forms a soft topping when baked and eliminates the need for icing.

½ cup sugar
½ cup warm milk
1 tablespoon butter or margarine, melted
2 egg yolks, well beaten
1 cup sifted all-purpose flour
1 teaspoon baking powder
½ teaspoon salt

Mix the sugar, warm milk and butter or margarine together. Add the egg yolks, then the dry ingredients and beat until light. Put in a well-greased 9-inch square pan, spread with Topping (see below), and bake 30 to 35 minutes in a 350°F oven.

TOPPING

2 egg whites
½ cup sugar
pinch salt
1 cup flaked coconut

Beat the egg whites until stiff, adding the sugar gradually while beating. Add the salt and coconut and spread on the cake before baking.

HOT MILK CAKE

A plain, light cake that goes very well with ice cream and sauces.

>2 eggs
>1 cup sugar
>1 teaspoon vanilla
>1 cup all-purpose flour
>1 teaspoon baking powder
>pinch salt
>½ cup milk
>2 teaspoons butter or margarine*

Beat the eggs and sugar until very light and add the vanilla. Sift together the flour, baking powder and salt.

Scald the milk and stir in the butter or margarine until melted.

Add the sifted ingredients alternately with the milk to the eggs and sugar.

Bake in a greased 9-inch square cake pan in a 350°F oven for 25 to 30 minutes. Split the cake and fill with English Lemon Curd (see page 182). Sprinkle the top with a dusting of confectioners' sugar.

*That's right — 2 *teaspoons.*

MYSTERY CAKE

So called because nobody can ever guess what's in it. Could you?

- 1 cup salad oil
- 2 cups sugar
- 4 eggs
- 2 cups all-purpose flour
- 2 teaspoons soda
- 2 teaspoons cinnamon
- 3 cups grated carrots
- 1 cup chopped nuts

Cream together the oil and sugar. Beat in the eggs. Sift together the flour, soda, and cinnamon and add. Beat 1½ minutes. Fold in the carrots and nuts. Bake in a greased loaf pan (9x5x2¾ inches) at 350°F for 1 hour. Frost when cool with White Gold Icing (see below).

WHITE GOLD ICING

- 1 8-ounce package cream cheese
- 4 tablespoons butter or margarine
- 1 pound confectioners' sugar
- 2 teaspoons vanilla

Soften the cream cheese and blend with the butter or margarine. Add the confectioners' sugar gradually. Add the vanilla. Frost the top and sides of the cake.

COOKIES

Cookies are for bribing little boys and girls, all of whom are cookie connoisseurs. So to make your mark you must use a *better* cookie. Ordinary cookies just won't do it.

How good are our recipes? Let us count the ways:

●

We remember one very small Cub Scout who, after feasting on our Fudge Meltaways, offered us his favorite jackknife, right on the spot, no strings attached.

Another young man, age six, solemnly ate his way through a handful of Sour Cream Chocolate Cookies without a word. Next day he was back with a shoebox full of what he considered to be his mother's best recipes.

And a little girl whose father ran a bakeshop was so crazy over the Russian Tea Cakes that she conned her father into giving us the recipe for the shop's very popular Fruit and Nut Cookies.

●

In fact, any of these cookies presented at the proper moment can get a lawn mowed, an attic emptied, a garage cleaned, a room tidied, a garden weeded. Or a little heart stolen.

CHEWY FRUIT AND NUT COOKIES

They have the added advantage of being very nourishing.

1¼ cups sifted all-purpose flour
¾ teaspoon baking soda
¾ teaspoon baking powder
½ teaspoon salt
½ teaspoon cinnamon
½ teaspoon ginger
½ cup soft butter or margarine
1 cup molasses
2 eggs, beaten
1½ cups rolled oats
1 cup golden raisins
1 cup chopped pecans
1 6-ounce package semi-sweet chocolate
   bits (optional)

Sift the flour, baking soda, baking powder, salt and spices together into a mixing bowl. Add the remaining ingredients. Beat at low speed of the electric mixer or by hand until well blended.

Use 2 teaspoons dough for each cookie; place well apart on ungreased cookie sheets and bake at 350°F for 10 to 12 minutes.   *Makes 3 dozen.*

CHINESE CHEWS

So easy a child can make them.

½ cup butter
1 cup firmly packed brown sugar
2 eggs
½ cup chopped mixed nuts
¼ cup dates, chopped

1 tablespoon chopped seedless raisins
1 tablespoon coconut
¾ cup sifted all-purpose flour

Cream the butter and sugar until fluffy. Beat the eggs and add them. Stir in the nuts, dates, raisins and coconut. Mix well. Add the flour and beat until blended.

Bake in an 8x8-inch greased pan for 40 minutes at 350°F. Cut into bars while warm. *Makes about 16 bars.*

SOUR CREAM CHOCOLATE COOKIES

Deliciously soft and munchy.

2 cups sifted cake flour
¼ teaspoon salt
½ teaspoon soda
2 teaspoons baking powder
½ cup butter or margarine
1 cup brown sugar, packed
1 egg
2 squares chocolate, melted and slightly
  cooled
1 cup sour cream
1 teaspoon vanilla
1 cup coarsely chopped walnuts

Sift together the flour, salt, soda and baking powder. Cream the butter or margarine with the sugar until light and fluffy. Add the egg and beat thoroughly. Blend in the melted chocolate. Add the dry ingredients alternately with the sour cream, beating until smooth after each addition. Stir in the vanilla and nuts.

Drop by teaspoons on to a greased cookie sheet. Bake at 375°F about 10 to 12 minutes.

Makes 3 to 3½ dozen.

DREAM CAKE SQUARES

Quick, easy and practically fool-proof.

> 1 cup all-purpose flour
> ½ cup butter or margarine
> 2 tablespoons confectioners' sugar
> 2 eggs, beaten
> 1¼ cups light brown sugar
> 2 tablespoons all-purpose flour
> ½ teaspoon baking powder
> ½ teaspoon salt
> ½ cup walnuts, chopped
> ½ cup coconut

Mix the first three ingredients with your fingers. Press

into the bottom of an 11x7x1½-inch pan. Bake at 350°F for 15 minutes.

Mix together the rest of ingredients and pour over the baked base. Return to the oven for 30 minutes.

Makes 24 squares.

FUDGE MELTAWAYS

After you melt the chocolate and butter or margarine, all the rest of the "cooking" is done in the refrigerator.

½ cup butter or margarine
1 square unsweetened chocolate
¼ cup sugar
1 teaspoon vanilla
1 egg, beaten
2 cups graham cracker crumbs
1 cup coconut
½ cup chopped nuts
¼ cup butter
1 tablespoon milk
2 cups sifted confectioners' sugar
1 teaspoon vanilla
1½ squares unsweetened chocolate, melted

Melt the ½ cup butter or margarine and the 1 square chocolate in a saucepan. Add the sugar, vanilla, egg, graham cracker crumbs, coconut and nuts and mix thoroughly. Press into a 9x9-inch pan. Refrigerate.

Cream the ¼ cup butter with the milk, confectioners' sugar and vanilla. Spread over the crumb mixture. Chill in the refrigerator.

Pour melted chocolate over the chilled mixture in the pan and spread evenly. Store in the refrigerator. Cut into squares before firm.

Makes 16 squares.

RASPBERRY COCONUT SQUARES

Everybody loves the way these two great flavors come together.

> 1¾ cups all-purpose flour
> 1½ cups sugar, divided
> ¼ teaspoon salt
> ½ cup butter or margarine
> 4 eggs
> ½ cup seedless red raspberry jam
> ¼ cup butter or margarine, softened
> 1½ cups shredded coconut

Put the flour, ½ cup sugar and the salt in a mixing bowl and blend well. With a pastry blender, cut in the ½ cup butter or margarine until the particles are quite fine. Add 1 lightly beaten egg and toss to mix. Gather the mixture together, working quickly with your hands to form a dough. Press the mixture evenly on the bottom of a lightly buttered 10x15-inch pan. Spread the jam on top.

Cream the softened butter or margarine with the remaining 1 cup sugar. Add the remaining 3 eggs one at a time, beating after each addition. Beat until light and creamy. Add the coconut and mix well. Spread over the jam layer.

Bake at 350°F for 20 to 25 minutes or until golden brown. Cool the pan on a rack. Cut in squares.

Makes 36 squares.

RUSSIAN TEA CAKES

"What are those little round things?"

1 cup soft butter
½ cup confectioners' sugar
1 teaspoon vanilla
2½ cups sifted all-purpose flour
½ teaspoon salt
¾ cup finely chopped walnuts

Cream the butter and sugar. Add the vanilla. Sift the flour and salt together and stir in. Mix in the nuts.

Chill the dough. Roll into 1-inch balls. Place 2½ inches apart on an ungreased baking sheet. Bake until set, but not brown, in a 350°F oven for 10 to 12 minutes.

While still warm, roll in confectioners' sugar. Cool. Roll in the sugar once more. *Makes 4 dozen.*

12
DESSERTS

The old-fashioned, heavy dessert has fallen into disfavor since it became wise to count calories and cholesterol. But that's no reason to renounce dessert completely and deny your table what many consider to be one of its greatest pleasures.

A good meal deserves a fitting finale and no menu is really complete without one. So don't wonder *if* you should have dessert. Just decide *what*.

Apply the same logic in planning desserts as you do to soups and appetizers; if the meal is heavy in the middle, then make it light on both ends. Don't serve mince pie and ice cream after roast beef and Yorkshire pudding. Try fruit in wine. After a light dinner of salad and fish, *then* you can bring on the cakes and éclairs.

So always plan a dessert of some kind. You deserve it. You ate your vegetables, didn't you? Besides, it isn't until the coffee and dessert are served that the good conversation begins.

And that's the best part of any meal.

APPLE COBBLER

The time to make this all-American dessert is in the fall, when you can get apples that are crisp and snappy.

1 cup sugar
2 tablespoons cornstarch
¼ teaspoon cinnamon
1 cup water
2 tablespoons butter or margarine
5 cups apples, peeled and thinly sliced
1 cup all-purpose flour
1½ teaspoons baking powder
½ teaspoon salt
4 tablespoons sugar, divided
2 tablespoons butter or margarine
¼ cup cold water
2 teaspoons grated orange peel

Blend 1 cup sugar with the cornstarch and cinnamon in a large saucepan. Add the water. Bring to a boil, stirring constantly. Add 2 tablespoons butter or margarine and the apples to the hot sauce. Pour into a shallow baking dish.

In a mixing bowl, combine the baking powder, salt and 2 tablespoons sugar with the flour. Cut in the additional 2 tablespoons butter or margarine. Add the cold water and stir with a fork to soft dough. Smooth the dough into a ball on a floured board. Knead five or six times. Roll out ½ inch thick. Cut with a 2½-inch cookie cutter, then cut each piece in half. Arrange around the baking dish.

Combine the remaining 2 tablespoons sugar and the orange peel. Sprinkle on the dough. Bake in a 450°F oven for 25 minutes, or until the apples are tender and the biscuits golden brown. Serve with sweetened whipped cream. *Serves 6.*

BAKED GINGERED BANANAS

In which you turn a very ordinary banana into a very glamorous dessert.

 6 bananas, a little underripe
 2 tablespoons butter or margarine
 ¼ cup maple syrup
 2 tablespoons shaved crystallized ginger

Peel the bananas and slice in half, lengthwise. Place in a single layer in a greased baking dish. Pour the maple syrup over them and dot with butter or margarine. Bake in a 375°F oven for 30 minutes, turning after 15 minutes.

Serve with crystallized ginger sprinkled on each portion. *Serves 6.*

BLUEBERRY BETTY

Don't be tempted to make this with anything but fresh blueberries.

 4 cups fresh blueberries
 3 tablespoons melted butter or
   margarine
 2 cups fresh bread crumbs
 ½ cup brown sugar
 1 teaspoon cinnamon
 1 tablespoon grated lemon rind
 2 tablespoons lemon juice
 ¼ cup hot water

Rinse the blueberries and drain well. Toss melted butter or margarine with the crumbs. Combine the sugar, cinnamon and lemon rind.

Sprinkle one-third of the bread crumbs in the bottom of a well-buttered 1½-quart baking dish. Cover with half the drained blueberries and sprinkle with half the sugar mixture. Repeat — crumbs, blueberries and sugar. Top with the last third of the crumbs.

Combine the lemon juice and hot water and pour evenly over the top. Bake at 350°F for 30 minutes.

Serve warm with sweetened whipped cream. *Serves 6.*

BUTTERSCOTCH NUT PUDDING

A good dessert to serve when the main course is a light one.

> 2 tablespoons butter or margarine
> ½ cup white sugar
> 1 cup milk or light cream
> 1 cup sifted all-purpose flour
> 2 teaspoons baking powder
> ½ teaspoon salt
> ½ cup raisins
> ⅓ cup chopped walnuts
> 2 cups lukewarm water
> 1 cup brown sugar
> 1 tablespoon butter
> 1 tablespoon cornstarch

Cream the 2 tablespoons butter or margarine with the

½ cup of white sugar. Add to this the milk or cream, flour, baking powder, salt, raisins and nuts.

Mix the water, brown sugar, butter, and cornstarch. Boil for 5 minutes.

Grease a 2-quart casserole. Pour in the syrup first, then spread the batter over it. Bake for 1 hour at 350°F.

Serve warm with whipped cream.   *Serves 6.*

CHERRIES JUBILEE

There is no more elegant or dramatic finale to a meal than a flaming dessert done right at the table, and anybody who aspires to gourmet-cook status should learn how to do one. Cherries Jubilee is easy. All you need is a can of cherries, some ice cream and a little liquor.

1 1-pound can dark sweet pitted cherries
1 tablespoon cornstarch
2 tablespoons sugar
pinch salt
1 tablespoon lemon juice
¼ cup brandy, or any fruit liqueur over
   60 proof
1 quart vanilla ice cream

Drain the cherries, reserving ½ cup of the syrup. Put this syrup in a chafing dish and add the cornstarch, sugar and salt. Simmer, stirring occasionally, until the liquid is smooth and thick. Remove from the heat and stir in the cherries and lemon juice. (Do this in kitchen.)

When ready to serve at the table, put the chafing dish with contents on its stand over a candle or alcohol burner and heat, stirring gently. Add the brandy or liqueur and ignite*. Keep stirring until the flames begin to die down, then ladle the fruit and sauce over the ice cream, which you have divided into four individual serving dishes.

Serves 4.

*NOTE: When you flambé, exercise sensible safety precautions. Keep away from drapes and curtains. Don't let guests lean too close. It may be well to practice a couple of times, alone, in the kitchen, before you go on stage.

For the ultimate in visual effect, keep the lights down low. Alcohol burns with a dark blue flame which isn't too visible in a bright room.

CHOCOLATE SOUFFLE

Rich and elegantly extravagant.

3 tablespoons butter or margarine
⅓ cup flour
⅓ cup sugar
1 cup light cream
3 egg yolks, well-beaten
2 squares unsweetened chocolate
½ teaspoon vanilla
4 egg whites
whipped cream, lightly sweetened

Melt the butter, blend in the flour and sugar, and mix well. Add the cream. Cook, stirring, over medium heat until thick. Beat a small amount of the hot mixture into the egg yolks. Return to the saucepan, blend well and cook 1 minute longer. Cool slightly.

Stir in the chocolate which has been melted over hot water. Add the vanilla. Beat the egg whites until stiff but not dry. Fold into the chocolate mixture.

Butter a 1½-quart soufflé dish and sprinkle with granulated sugar. Spoon the mixture into the dish and set in a pan containing 1½ inches of hot water. Bake in a 350°F oven for about 30 minutes or until firm.

Serve at once with whipped cream. *Serves 6.*

COTTAGE PUDDING WITH NUTMEG SAUCE

Here's a real, old-fashioned dish that your family will like just as much as ours does. Try to use freshly grated nutmeg.

⅓ cup soft butter or margarine
1¼ cups sugar
1 egg
1¾ cups sifted all-purpose flour
3 teaspoons baking powder
1 teaspoon salt
1 cup milk
1 teaspoon lemon flavoring

Cream the butter or margarine with the sugar and egg. Add the sifted dry ingredients alternately with the milk. Beat for 2 minutes. Add the flavoring. Bake in an 8-inch greased pan for 25 minutes in a 375°F oven.

Serve warm with Nutmeg Sauce (see below). *Serves 6.*

NUTMEG SAUCE

1 cup sugar
1 cup water
1 tablespoon cornstarch
2 tablespoons butter or margarine
1 teaspoon freshly grated nutmeg

Combine the sugar and cornstarch and blend with the water. Cook in a double boiler over hot water, stirring until thickened. Remove from the heat and stir in the butter or margarine and nutmeg. Serve hot.

DESSERT CREME

A light dessert, suitable for luncheon or after a heavy meal.

      2 envelopes unflavored gelatin
      4 cups milk
      4 eggs, separated
      ¾ cup sugar
      ¼ teaspoon salt
      1 teaspoon vanilla

Soak the gelatin in cold milk in the top of a double boiler for 5 minutes. Heat over boiling water until the gelatin is dissolved. Beat the egg yolks slightly with a rotary beater. Add ¼ cup of the sugar and the salt. Add a small amount of the hot milk and mix well.

Add the egg mixture to the double boiler and cook, stirring constantly, for 2 or 3 minutes or until the mixture coats the spoon.

Let stand until cold, then chill until slightly thickened. Beat the egg whites until foamy; then add to them the re-

maining ½ cup sugar gradually and continue beating until stiff but not dry. Fold in the gelatin mixture. Stir in the vanilla and pour into eight parfait glasses.

Chill until firm and serve garnished with fresh strawberries, raspberries or peaches. *Serves 8.*

ENGLISH TRIFLE

An English classic. If there's such a thing as leftover cake, this is what you make with it.

> 1 cup dry unfrosted cake cubes
> 2 tablespoons cream sherry
> ½ cup raspberry jam
> 1 cup soft custard
> 1 cup whipping cream

Put the cake in a serving bowl and sprinkle with the sherry. Spread with raspberry jam. Pour Soft Custard (see below) all over.

Whip the cream until stiff and serve with the Trifle.

Serves 6.

SOFT CUSTARD

> 1 cup milk
> 3 egg yolks
> 2 tablespoons brown sugar
> pinch salt
> ½ teaspoon almond flavoring

Scald the milk in the top of a double boiler. Blend a small amount of the hot milk with the beaten egg yolks. Stir this mixture into the rest of the milk. Cook and stir over hot, but not boiling, water until the custard coats a spoon (about 6 minutes). Add the salt, sugar and flavoring. Chill.

FLOATING ISLANDS

Really light — just right to top off a heavy meal.

> ¼ teaspoon salt, divided
> 3 egg whites
> 10 tablespoons sugar, divided
> 1½ cups milk
> ½ cup light cream
> 6 egg yolks
> 1¼ teaspoons vanilla

Add ⅛ teaspoon salt to the egg whites and beat until foamy. Add 6 tablespoons sugar gradually and continue beating until stiff. Drop heaping tablespoonsful of this into ½ inch of boiling water in a shallow baking pan. Bake in a moderate oven (325°F) for 10 minutes. Remove carefully from the water with a spatula or slotted spoon and let stand on a cake rack until cold.

Scald the milk and cream in the top of a double boiler. Beat the egg yolks; add ⅛ teaspoon salt and 4 tablespoons sugar. Mix in a little of the hot milk and cream with the eggs and return to the double boiler. Cook until thick, stirring constantly. Cool. Add the vanilla and chill.

Serve in shallow glass dessert dishes with the egg-white "islands" floating on top.   *Serves 4.*

LEMON SOUFFLE PUDDING

After you make this, you'll find a thick liquid on the bottom which makes a great sauce.

> 1½ cups sugar
> ⅛ teaspoon salt
> 2½ tablespoons flour
> 2½ tablespoons butter
> 2½ lemons, juice and rinds
> 3 eggs, separated

1 extra egg white
1¼ cups milk

Mix the sugar, salt and flour. Add the butter, lemon juice, rind and beaten egg yolks, blended with the milk. Beat well.

Fold in the stiffly beaten egg whites.

Pour into a buttered casserole, place in a pan of hot, but not boiling, water and bake for 30 minutes in a 350°F oven.

When you serve the pudding, spoon the liquid on the bottom over it as a sauce. *Serves 6.*

CHILLED LEMON SOUFFLE

A fantastic dessert that you'll want to learn to do well — and serve at formal dinner parties.

1 envelope unflavored gelatin
2 tablespoons water
grated rind of 4 lemons
½ cup fresh lemon juice
1 cup sugar, divided
1 cup egg whites (about 8)
1 cup heavy cream
1 lemon, sliced paper thin

Dissolve the gelatin in 2 tablespoons water. Add the lemon rind and juice and ½ cup sugar. Place in a saucepan and stir over low heat until the gelatin is thoroughly dissolved; then chill to syrup consistency.

Beat the egg whites until foamy and add ½ cup sugar gradually until smooth and stiff. Beat in the gelatin mixture.

Whip the cream and fold in.

Pour into 10-inch spring-form pan. Press the lemon slices gently onto surface to decorate. Chill for 8 hours and serve in wedges. *Serves 12.*

MAPLE CHARLOTTE

A must for this recipe is pure maple syrup.

> 1 tablespoon unflavored gelatin
> ¼ cup water
> 2 cups milk
> 3 eggs, separated
> ⅛ teaspoon salt
> 1 cup pure maple syrup

Dissolve the gelatin in the water. Put the milk in a double boiler and sprinkle the dissolved gelatin on top. Heat to scalding, stirring until gelatin dissolves entirely.

Beat the egg yolks with salt, stirring in half the milk slowly. Return all to the double boiler and cook over hot (not boiling) water until the mixture coats the spoon.

Remove from the heat, stir in the maple syrup, and cool until the mixture thickens. Then whip until light and frothy. Beat the egg whites stiff, and fold into the syrup and egg mixture. Chill until firm. *Serves 6.*

MAPLE SYRUP SUNDAE SAUCE

Quote from a professional dessert-lover: "If I had to live with just one dessert, this is the one it would be."

1¼ cups pure maple syrup
1 cup sugar
¼ teaspoon salt
½ cup heavy cream
2 tablespoons butter

Combine all the ingredients in a medium saucepan, stirring constantly, until the mixture comes to a boil. Simmer, uncovered, for 5 minutes, stirring occasionally. Cool slightly, and serve warm, over your favorite ice cream. *Makes 2 cups.*

SOUR CREAM ORANGE SAUCE

An easy way to make a nice dessert out of a plain piece of cake.

¼ cup butter
½ cup confectioners' sugar
⅓ cup sour cream
3 tablespoons fresh orange juice
1½ teaspoons grated orange rind

Cream softened butter with confectioners' sugar. Beat in the sour cream, orange juice and rind.
Serve with slices of any plain cake. *Makes 1 cup.*

BRANDIED PEACH ICE

This masterpiece was created by the Executive Chef of a very famous hotel, who refused to give the recipe to even his best friends. We enjoyed it so many times that we were finally able to reconstruct it well enough that nobody (including the Executive Chef) could tell the difference between ours and the original.

2 cups ripe, peeled and chopped peaches
1 cup sugar
2 tablespoons brandy, divided
2 cups light cream
2 teaspoons unflavored gelatin
¼ cup cold water
1 cup heavy cream, whipped

Mix the peaches and sugar and let stand for 30 minutes. Force the mixture through a sieve, add 1 tablespoon brandy and stir in the 2 cups light cream.

Sprinkle the 2 teaspoons gelatin over the ¼ cup cold water. Dissolve over hot water. Stir into the peaches and cream mixture. Pour into covered molds or refrigerator trays covered with foil and place in the freezer. While still soft, beat twice at half hour intervals to reduce the size of the crystals. Whip the heavy cream, add the remaining tablespoon brandy and fold the whipped cream into the ice after the last beating. Return to the freezer.

Remove from the freezer about 20 minutes before serving. Beat once more and pile into eight champagne glasses.   *Serves 8.*

PEACH MELBA

This is the way to make a true Peach Melba — with fresh fruit.

1 cup sugar
1 cup water
1 teaspoon vanilla

3 large, fresh, yellow peaches
1 pint ripe raspberries
¼ cup sugar
1 quart French vanilla ice cream

Combine the sugar and water. Bring to the boiling point, stirring constantly. Lower the heat, cover, and boil over medium heat for 7 minutes. Remove from heat and add the vanilla.

Drop the peaches into boiling water for 1 or 2 minutes, then peel. Cut into halves, removing the pits.

Over medium heat, add two peach halves at once to the syrup, and poach 3 minutes. Remove from the syrup with a slotted spoon and chill.

Press the raspberries through a food mill or purée in the blender. Stir in ¼ cup sugar. Chill.

Put a serving of ice cream in six glass dessert dishes, place the peaches on top, cut side down. Spoon the purée over the peaches. *Serves 6.*

POTS DE CREME AU CHOCOLAT

A classic French dessert to add to your repertoire. This one is really quite easy to make.

13 ounces sweet dark chocolate
½ cup double strength coffee
2 teaspoons brandy
6 egg yolks
6 egg whites
½ cup grated blanched almonds

Melt the chocolate in a double boiler with the coffee. Stir until smooth, remove from the heat and add the brandy. Cool slightly. Add the egg yolks, one at a time, mixing well after each one.

Beat the egg whites until stiff and fold into the egg and chocolate mixture until the whites disappear.

Pour into little covered pots or demi-tasse cups and sprinkle with grated almonds. Chill for 2 hours. *Serves 8.*

OLD-FASHIONED RICE PUDDING

Don't confuse this with any other rice pudding you ever had. This old English recipe is rich and luscious, and everyone in your family will love it.

    1 quart milk
    ½ cup sugar
    ¼ cup uncooked brown rice
    ½ teaspoon salt
    1 teaspoon vanilla
    ⅛ teaspoon nutmeg

Mix all the ingredients together and put in a casserole. Bake, uncovered, for 3 hours in a 300°F oven.

During the first hour, stir the pudding every 20 minutes.

Serve with a lacing of cream. *Serves 6.*

STRAWBERRIES ROMANOFF *or* RASPBERRIES ROMANOFF

This is the dessert we choose to make on very special occasions. It's fabulous and always makes a big impression, especially when you put it together right at the table. Don't make it unless you have either fresh strawberries or fresh raspberries.

    1 pint French vanilla ice cream
    1 cup heavy cream, whipped
    4 tablespoons Grand Marnier liqueur
    1 quart fresh strawberries or raspberries

Soften the ice cream and fold the whipped cream into it. Add the Grand Marnier. Serve the berries in individual dessert dishes and pour the mixture over them.

Serves 6.

TOFFEE SAUCE PUDDING

Very rich — and it makes its own sauce.

1½ cups sifted all-purpose flour
2 teaspoons baking powder
1 teaspoon salt
½ cup butter or margarine, divided
⅔ cup sugar
1 cup milk
½ cup seedless raisins
1 lemon, grated peel and juice
½ cup light molasses
1¼ cups water

Mix and sift the flour, baking powder and salt. Cream 4 tablespoons of the butter with the sugar, added gradually. Cream until light and fluffy. Add the milk alternately with the flour mixture, beating until smooth after each addition. Stir in the raisins and lemon peel.

Spoon into a well-greased 9-inch square baking pan.

Combine the lemon juice with the remaining butter or margarine, the molasses and the water in a saucepan. Bring to a boil. Remove from heat; pour gently and evenly over batter. Bake at 350°F for 45 to 50 minutes.

To serve, spoon into dessert dishes and cover with sauce from the bottom of the baking pan.   *Serves 8.*

ENVOI

Here's where we get one-up and give you something you won't find in other cookbooks, at least none of the cookbooks we've read. We're going to say "goodbye" and "thanks."

We're glad you have our book and we hope you enjoy it. Writing it was the hardest work we ever did.

Gamblers are warned to "quit while they're ahead."

Comedians are advised to "leave 'em laughing."

Politicians always try to "end on a positive note."

What should a cookbook-writer do ... "exit on an entrée?"

That's it.

INDEX

216

220